DESTINATION DARDANELLES

By the same author:

Baltic Assignment: British Submarines in Russia 1914–1919

DESTINATION DARDANELLES

Michael Wilson

LEO COOPER
LONDON

First published 1988 by Leo Cooper Ltd

Leo Cooper is an independent imprint of
the Heinemann Group of Publishers,
10 Upper Grosvenor Street, London W1X 9PA.

LONDON   MELBOURNE   JOHANNESBURG   AUCKLAND

Printed and bound in Great Britain by
Mackays of Chatham

The Naval History of Britain contains no page more wonderful than that which describes the prowess of her submarines at the Dardanelles. Their exploits constitute the finest example of submarine warfare in the whole of the Great War.

Winston S Churchill.

Contents

Illustrations

ILLUSTRATIONS

MAPS
Drawn by Patrick Leeson

TABLES

ACKNOWLEDGEMENTS

The author and publishers would like to thank the following for
permission to reproduce copyright photographs: The Submarine
Museum, Nos 1, 4, 5, 6, 8, 11, 16, 17, 18, 20 and 22; Mr B. Head,
No 2; The Countess of Elgin, No 3; Mr D. Hallifax and the Imperial
War Museum, Nos 7, 9 and 19; Mr Rene Gregor, Nos 12 and 13; Mr
Peter Haywood, Nos 14 and 15; the Fleet Air Arm Museum, No 10;
the Imperial War Museum, No 21.

Preface

THE KEEPING OF DIARIES by members of the armed forces in time of war is forbidden, a ruling which is, I suspect, common to other countries as well as Britain. Yet, after a war these diaries surface by the score to form the basis of the memoirs of the famous and the not so famous. Others gather dust in attics while waiting for an interested son or grandson to rediscover them. But where would historians be without them? They provide a factual account of the events of the time as seen by the author undisturbed by hindsight. Being essentially private they tend to be uninhibited, while omissions are those of lack of knowledge rather than in answer to any call for a cover-up. On the other hand it must not be forgotten that the picture they paint is that seen by the writer who may not be privy to the wider scene of strategy and tactics, or even events in a neighbouring ship or batallion.

This is the story of one young naval officer's war for thirteen months from its outbreak in August, 1914. Since he was serving in the submarine HMS *E7* it is essentially the story of that submarine. For eight months they faced the boredom, dangers and winter weather of the Heligoland Bight at a time when the operation of submarines in war was new and tactics were discovered and developed by experience. It was a time when the British Grand Fleet and German High Seas Fleet sought to find the other's weakness which could lead to an outright victory on the scale of Trafalgar.

Lieutenant Oswald Hallifax and the *E7* then found themselves sent to the Mediterranean to support the ill-fated Gallipoli campaign, destined to force the Dardanelles and operate in the Sea of Marmara. There they and the other British and French submarines were instructed to interrupt the flow of Turkish sea-borne supplies to the front, a submarine success story which has become one of the classics of submarine warfare.

Above all it is the story of submariners fighting a war with a new weapon which few recognized for its potential or perceived its way of operating.

This story would not have been possible without the diaries of Lieutenant Oswald Hallifax. I am indebted to his son, the late Mr Derek Hallifax, for his kind permission to quote extensively from these diaries, the originals of which are kept by the Imperial War Museum, with copies at the RN Submarine Museum at Gosport. I am also grateful to Derek's widow, Mrs Jean Hallifax, his sister Mrs C. Samuel, and his nephew Mr J. Westwood for their subsequent support.

I also wish to thank Mr Douglas Cochrane and his wife for their hospitality and the time taken to talk to me about his father, the late Captain Sir Archibald Cochrane; also the Dowager Countess of Elgin, Captain Cochrane's sister.

Mr Gus Britton of the staff of the RN Submarine Museum has always been a great help and encouragement. His expertise is thankfully acknowledged. I also wish to thank Commander Richard Compton-Hall, the Director of the Museum, for allowing me to use the Museum facilities and for permission to use some of the Museum's many photographs.

My thanks also to Mrs Ursula Betts for permission to use the verses from the poem *Hang On* written by her father, Commander J. G. Bower, which are quoted in Chapter 5; to Mrs B. Favell for permission to quote from the diary of her father, Commander (later Vice-Admiral Sir) Cecil Talbot; this diary too is now held by the Imperial War Museum; to Century Hutchinson Ltd for the use made of material originally published by them in 1928 in *The Uncensored Dardanelles* by E. Ashmead-Bartlett; to the Controller of Her Majesty's Stationery Office for the use of Crown Copywright material in the Public Record Office; and to Rear Admiral J. R. Hill for permission to quote from the *Naval Review*. I am most grateful to those who have loaned me photographs and given permission for their use.

Others who have aided my research and whose help is gratefully acknowledged include Mr Rod Suddaby of the Imperial War Museum;

Mr Brian Head who has given so much assistance particularly as a result of his own work on the story of HMS *E31* and Lieutenant Commander Feilmann; Mr Tony Vine of the Royal Australian Navy; Mr Graham Mottram of the Fleet Air Arm Museum; Mr 'Seb' Cox of the Air Historical Branch of the Ministry of Defence; Mr Alexander Cochrane whose book *The Fighting Cochranes* provided so many leads; Lieutenant-Commander Arnold Hague RNR, Mr David Lees and Mr Tom Adams of the World Ship Society; and finally, but by no means least, Mr Alan Francis of the Naval Historical Library in the Ministry of Defence whose willing help solved so many problems.

1
Introduction

SINCE THE MIDDLE AGES many inventors in Europe, and later in America, had experimented with submersibles, that is ships which could travel under the sea as well as on the surface. Indeed it was man's greatest desire either to be able to fly like the birds or to be able to travel in the sea like the fishes. But the true development of the submarine needed the impetus of two other technological advances: a satisfactory engine to propel the boat underwater, and a weapon that would justify the use of a submarine against an enemy but which would give the submarine itself a chance to survive the attack. Both these advances came in the closing years of the nineteenth century with the successful development of Whitehead's self-propelled torpedo in 1868 and the installation of an electric motor in a submarine by a Spanish naval officer in 1886.

By the end of the century the French were establishing themselves as the leading submarine power. The fact that such a force was just across the Channel from the main naval base at Portsmouth was not lost on the Admiralty for, despite the improving political relations that were to lead within a few years to the *Entente Cordiale*, there remained a traditional suspicion of the French surviving from centuries of warfare. It was this suspicion that finally led the Admiralty to look seriously at the requirement for submarine development in the Royal Navy.

Visiting England from America in the summer of 1900 was Mr Isaac Rice of the Electric Boat company who had built the first submarine for the US Navy and was then preparing to build seven more of a slightly improved design. The design came from John Phillip Holland who had emigrated from Ireland to America in 1873 and then produced, with no official support, a series of submarines each larger than its predecessor and of varying viability, culminating in the one purchased by the Navy and named after him. As a result of Rice's visit it was agreed that Messrs Vickers Son & Maxim at Barrow would build five submarines for the Royal Navy on behalf of the American Company, the boats to be repeats of those being built in America.

It was a radical change of policy for the Admiralty who had been so firmly set against submarine development for so long. It may be partly excused, for it was stated in the following Naval Estimates that the submarines were being built so as to allow our destroyer commanding officers the opportunity of working against them.

A firm order was placed with Vickers in December, 1900, and Captain R. H. S. Bacon, a torpedo specialist, was sent to Barrow to oversee the work of construction. Lieutenant F. D. Arnold-Foster, another torpedo specialist, followed, destined to become the first commanding officer of the Royal Navy's first submarine. At Barrow the work of building this new vessel was carried on in great secrecy; Arnold-Foster recalls that on arrival in the shipyard he was anxious to sight his new ship but no one seemed to have heard of any submarine being built. Eventually the boat was found in a large shed prominently marked 'Yacht Shed', while parts were made and delivered as 'Pontoon Number One'.

Submarine Torpedo Boat No 1, or *Holland 1* as she became known, was launched without the usual ceremonies on 2 October, 1901, and began sea trials on 15 January the following year. The other boats followed in quick succession. The submarine as a vessel of war had now taken its place in the Royal Navy, but what sort of boats were these early submarines?

The *Holland* class were single-hulled vessels of spindle form, that is the main ballast tanks which were filled with water to make the submarine dive were internal to the pressure hull, and the hull itself was circular in shape with the centre of all sections in a straight line. At the forward end there was a single 18in torpedo tube. There were no internal watertight bulkheads, nor any provision for crew comfort; the cluttered interior was devoted solely to the working of the submarine. A 60-cell battery powered a single electric motor giving the submarine a nominal range of 25 miles at the maximum underwater speed of about 7 knots. On the surface a 4-cylinder petrol engine was expected to give a range of some 250 miles at the maximum speed of 8 knots, and was also used to charge the battery. A single rudder was fitted and there was one set of horizontal diving rudders to control the depth of the submarine. When on the surface there was little freeboard and even in a small sea there was the threat of foundering if the hatches were not kept shut. The problem of surface navigation was not helped by the small deck casing and the almost complete absence of what was later to be called a conning tower. The diving time was a matter of a few minutes depending on the amount of reserve buoyancy in the submarine when running on the surface - they were rarely kept in diving trim.

Earlier submarines like those in the French Navy had no periscope for submerged navigation and had to porpoise to the surface for the Commanding Officer to see through glass ports fitted to the side of the hull or in a cupola over the hatch. Even the *Hollands* when laid down had no such provision, and it was due to the work of Captain Bacon that they went to sea with an "optical tube". It was called a Unifocal Ball Joint type and stowed horizontally along the hull, being raised about a ball joint by hand. Once raised it could be trained, again by hand. For the user it had the disadvantage that, whilst objects seen ahead were seen in their normal posture, those astern were inverted, while those on the beam were on their sides! Primitive though this may sound, it was an advantage over no periscope at all and it is said that some officers claimed that they thereby gained an instant impression of the relative bearing of the object in view merely from its angle to the vertical. This arrangement did not last long.

Successive Inspecting Captains of Submarines ensured that the Admiralty kept up a steady programme of building and development with provision for new construction being included in the yearly Naval Estimates. After the *Hollands*, thirteen of the A class were built, followed in turn by the B and C classes, each progressively larger than the other. With the advent of the C class the surface displacement had risen from the *Hollands'* 104 tons to 290 tons, and the length from about 100 feet to 135 feet. Even so these boats were still essentially for defensive operations round the coast of the British Isles.

The first big change came in 1906 with the ordering of the first of the D class. In the *D1* the surface displacement was nearly double that of the earlier C class, but, more important, she was fitted with two diesel engines driving twin propellers. This was the first of what came to be known as "Overseas" submarines, capable of operating off an enemy shore. In this class the main ballast tanks were no longer fitted internal to the pressure hull but had become saddle tanks running along the outside of the hull, the space thus gained being available to increase the fuel capacity and to improve the habitability. Even so, any improvement in the habitability was marginal, for the crew had increased to a total of twenty-six and additional equipment also competed for any space available. There was no comfort, even sleeping space having to be found by the sailors where they could, and this in a boat intended for offshore work.

The Germans were even later than the British in adopting the submarine as a weapon of war. Admiral von Tirpitz, like so many of his British contemporaries, was firmly against the building of submarines and considered that his prime duty lay in building a big-ship navy to match that of Great Britain. The first submarines built in Germany were sold to the Russians and although the *U1* was ordered for the German Navy in December 1904, von Tirpitz had only weakened under strong pressure and remained unconvinced of their value.

Much of the drive necessary to ensure a regular new construction programme of submarines came from Admiral Sir John ("Jackie") Fisher who was the First Sea Lord until he retired in 1910. Jackie Fisher is more usually remembered for the introduction of the *Dreadnought*, the battleship which revolutionized the surface battle fleets of the world's navies, but he also ensured that the Royal Navy did not lag behind in submarine construction. His successor was Admiral Sir Arthur Wilson, perhaps better known for his bravery on land during the campaign against the Dervishes in the Sudan where he won the Victoria Cross. As early as 1901, when Controller of the Navy and so responsible for warship construction, he had called the submarine "a damned un-English weapon" and suggested that in wartime the crews of all submarines captured should be treated as pirates and hanged. It was the performance of the new *D1* that now so impressed the new First Sea Lord. During Fleet manoeuvres the submarine had proceeded unaccompanied from Portsmouth to the west coast of Scotland and then "sunk" two cruisers of the "enemy" fleet. As a result Sir Arthur felt that the development of the submarine must be in the hands of an officer who would ensure that this offensive spirit was continued. He appointed Roger Keyes as the next Inspecting Captain of Submarines.

Keyes was no submariner and had little or no knowledge of how they worked, except at second hand from his younger brother, Adrian, one of the first submariners. By his own admission he had no great ability in technical matters and was not even a torpedo specialist. Nevertheless, he was known for his great energy and charisma, two factors which he employed to the full during his long and controversial period as Inspecting Captain, during both peace and war.

Developing a proven design is often regarded as a safer way forward than trying a plethora of new designs, and the E class arrived as part of that natural progression and improvement. Provision was made for the first six of this new class in the 1910/11 Estimates, the first two being laid down in Chatham Dockyard in February, 1911. They were only marginally larger than the D class, displacing an extra 150 tons when on the surface, but the main difference lay in the arrangement of the torpedo tubes. Whereas the D class had three 18in torpedo tubes, two in the bow mounted one above the other and one in the stern, the E class had four. These were fitted one each in the bow and stern and two amidships, one firing on either beam. At the time the E class were being designed there was a strong feeling among submariners against bow tubes for they felt that as submarines became longer it was becoming more difficult to manoeuvre clear of the target after firing torpedoes at the short ranges then necessary for success. Because of these fears the amidships tubes were introduced in the E class, and at one time the omission of any tube in the bow was seriously considered.

In 1900 the American Admiral O'Neil, referring to the US Navy's first submarine, said that "the only use of the *Holland* is to discharge torpedoes, and no weapon is more erratic". The coming war years were to demonstrate just how erratic the torpedo could be, and for many submarines it was their only weapon. British submarines carried no other weapon until the *D4*, which was fitted experimentally with a 12-pounder gun which could be retracted into the casing. Even so, it was not until after the outbreak of war in 1914 that the practice of fitting a gun became more general and the *E7*, like the other early boats of her class, was completed without a gun. Then many vintage guns of varying calibres were brought out of store to be fitted, some being of almost greater age than the submarines' youthful commanding officers. Commander Cromie, when in the *E19* in the Baltic, had a 6-pounder gun made in 1897. After one action he wrote that the

5

bore was then quite smooth and the shells could be seen tumbling through the air.

On the morning of 30 March, 1912, in Chatham Dockyard work began on a new submarine which was launched on 2 October the following year as HMS *E7*. Just over five months later Lieutenant Ferdinand ("Ferdie") Eric Feilmann commissioned his new command. Feilmann was the son of a prosperous merchant and had been born in Calcutta in August, 1883. His early years had followed the same pattern of so many young boys born in India in the years before the Great War; after a boyhood in Calcutta surrounded by servants he returned to England for school. Then in January, 1898, at the age of 14, he entered the Royal Navy as a Cadet in HMS *Britannia*. The imposing Naval College which we know today and which dominates the lower reaches of the River Dart and the town of Dartmouth had not then been built. Future naval officers lived, learned and slept afloat, the establishment comprising the old line-of-battle ship *Britannia*, a picturesque relic of England's wooden walls built in 1860, while astern was moored the even older *Hindustan* with her upper deck roofed over to form classrooms, but still distinguishable as the second rate she had once been.

In those days for entrance to the Royal Navy it was necessary to secure a nomination, pass a medical examination and then take the competitive Civil Service entrance examination. Successful young men, who had to be between the ages of 14 and 15½ years, were then expected to complete four terms at Dartmouth before going on to join a ship of the Fleet. They were not paid, indeed their parents were expected to pay £25 a term towards the cost of their education – less than the cost of a Public School, so many parents may have considered this a bargain. Parents also had to contribute one shilling a week which was paid to the Cadet in the form of pocket money. Instruction was mainly in the subjects that were to be of use in the future such as Navigation and Seamanship with some Engineering, while the more usual academic subjects also figured in the curriculum. Two small ships, HMS *Wave* and *Racer*, were attached to the College to give the Cadets the chance of practical work at sea.

One of Feilmann's fellow cadets was Bertram Ramsay, who as Admiral Sir Bertram Ramsay masterminded the evacuation from Dunkirk in 1940 and the planning for the invasion in Normandy in 1944. During his first term Feilmann would have found among the more senior cadets one Andrew Cunningham, destined to make his name in both the coming wars. In command of the *Britannia* when Feilmann arrived was Captain the Hon A. G. Curzon-Howe, who had the reputation of being one of the politest and most punctilious officers in the Royal Navy. He was also strict. The Commander, or second in command, was Christopher Craddock who, sixteen years later, perished with his Squadron at the Battle of Coronel.

Feilmann did well at the college and achieved four months seniority on passing out, at which time he and Bertram Ramsay joined the cruiser HMS *Crescent* in May, 1899, for service on the North America and West Indies Station. Feilmann was promoted Midshipman in September of that year. In all, he served for just over three years in the *Crescent* which was, by all accounts, a happy and efficient ship in which the young midshipmen were given every opportunity to see and experience life in Canada and the other countries which the cruiser visited. Shortly after being promoted to Sub-Lieutenant he joined the smaller cruiser HMS *Charybdis*. It is interesting to note that four other young officers sharing the gunroom of the *Charybdis* with Feilmann were destined to become submarine commanding officers in the coming war; Clement Head (lost when the *D2* was sunk), Robert Chisholm (sunk in the *E37*), Fitzroy Byron and Charles Brodie, who was prominent as one of Keyes' staff officers during the Dardanelles Campaign. Who knows what talk of submarines there was among these shipmates, and who influenced whom in their choice of specialization?

It was in 1904, after his courses at the Royal Naval College at Greenwich where he gained further distinction, and then some service in destroyers, that Feilmann was appointed to HMS *Thames* for submarine training. Among his fellow students were Edward Boyle and Martin Nasmith, both destined to win the Victoria Cross in the coming conflict. As a young Lieutenant he was appointed to his first command the following year, one of the A class submarines. There followed the customary period back in General Service when he served for a year in each of the battleships *Russell* and *St Vincent*, command of two C class submarines and then his appointment to the *E7*.

It has been related how the periscopes of the early submarines had very poor vision, and, to add to the commanding officer's difficulties, when he trained the periscope on the beam, the horizon became vertical. When he looked astern the horizon was once again horizontal but the image was inverted. The sea was on top and any ships in sight appeared to be hanging down from the horizon. On one occasion, when in command of the *A4*, Feilmann was making an attack on a small submarine tender off the beach at Alverstoke, and, as was customary, the target ship was flying a large red flag. Struggling to get a view in the choppy sea conditions and with the target between the submarine and the beach Feilmann suddenly saw what he thought was the red flag. As his sights came on he fired his torpedo. Unfortunately the red flag was a large red parasol under which the wife of a retired Colonel was sitting on the beach. Feilmann's shot was perfect and the torpedo hit the beach and ran up alongside the terrified lady. Reputedly the irate Colonel threatened to sue both the Admiralty and Feilmann for damages!

From quite an early age Feilmann was a keen fencer and became a noted expert with the sabre. In 1907 he was British Amateur Sabre Champion, an event which was covered by *The Field*, which reported that Lieutenant Feilmann, who fences with more steadiness and judgement with the sabre than he does with the foil, and fought well in the preliminary round, gave promise of a close finish. At the Royal Tournament that year he took part in the sabre competition where 'fighting in excellent style he secured an easy victory, though undue impetuosity cost him one defeat in the final'. The following year Feilmann was selected to represent Great Britain with the sabre in the Olympic Games, but unfortunately was unable to take part due to service commitments – it would seem that the annual naval manoeuvres were regarded as of higher priority than the Olympic Games by Their Lordships of the Admiralty. *The Times*, in their coverage of the Games, said that the British team was placed at a serious disadvantage by the absence of Lieutenant Feilmann and Mr H. Evan James, two amateur ex-champions, the former being unable to obtain leave.

Captain Henry Crane, a contemporary of Feilmann, recalled a story that was apparently quite well known at the time. On a visit to Paris Ferdie was involved in an argument with a Frenchman who challenged him to a duel. Before the event took place the Frenchman visited his fencing master to brush up his technique. The latter naturally took a professional interest in such matters and enquired as to his pupil's opponent. On being told that it was Ferdinand Feilmann, the fencing master advised that the challenge be withdrawn and an apology made.

With such prowess in this sport Ferdie must have been very quick on his feet to make up for his short stature, but in later years Douglas Gavin, his First Lieutenant in the *E31*, recalls that he had become very rotund, so much so that when going through the conning tower hatch he effectively sealed the boat and the diesel engines would start to draw a vacuum!

An interest in amateur theatricals has always been a popular pastime in the Navy and in this Ferdie was no exception. A review published in the *Harwich and Dovercourt Standard* for 10 December, 1910, gives praise to Lieutenant Feilmann for his performance as a stage villain.

Those who knew him at the time recall that he was a great character, a loved "bachelor uncle" among the children who was frequently asked around to visit the families of his fellow submariners living in the area. His professional reports describe him as "zealous" and "possessing good and sound judgement". This then was the man who was chosen to command the new *E7*, by all appearances destined to make a good career, yet making the events to come all the harder to understand.

The First Lieutenant* of the new submarine was Lieutenant Oswald Ernest Hallifax. Unlike his commanding officer Hallifax came from a naval family. The fourth of eight children, he was born in Hampshire on 12 November, 1888, shortly after his father, John Salwey Hallifax, had been promoted Captain. Both his elder brothers were to serve in the Royal Navy, reaching flag rank and dying during the Second World War. A younger brother was to serve in the Royal Naval Air Service during the coming war.

Oswald Hallifax himself joined the Royal Navy as a cadet in January, 1904, going direct, as did Feilmann, to the *Britannia* at Dartmouth. While this method of entry still continued, and would do so until 1906, a new scheme had recently been started whereby boys were much younger when joining and would spend longer under training, partly at a new college at Osborne in the Isle of Wight and partly at Dartmouth. Among his contemporaries there were few destined to reach flag rank in the years to come; perhaps the casualty

---

* In the early days of submarines it was the custom to refer to a submarine commanding officer's principal assistant as the Second Captain, or Second Officer – known as Second Dickie to the crew. Additional officers then became known as the Third or Fourth Officer. The more usual term today is First Lieutenant, a term which is used here.

lists of Jutland and elsewhere were to cut short too many promising careers. Of those in his term who became submariners both Charles Moore and Leopold Scarlett were killed when the Australian *AE1* was mysteriously lost in the Pacific in the early days of the war. Another, Richard Pulleyne, survived the accidental sinking of the *B2* in 1912, to be awarded the DSO and the DSC before being lost when the *E34* was mined and sunk with all hands in 1918. A fourth, Alexander Greig, survived the war, having served in the *E8* in the Baltic where he was awarded both the DSC and the Russian Order of St Vladimir.

In May, 1905, with final examinations behind him, and two months' seniority gained on their result, Hallifax left the strict spartan existence of the College to join his first ships, initially HMS *Highflyer* and then *Commonwealth*. After the usual round of courses, more exams and time at sea he was promoted Lieutenant in December, 1910. The following October he joined HMS *Defence* and only days later the cruiser sailed for India with three others escorting Their Majesties the King and Queen who were on board the *SS Medina*.

Hallifax began his submarine training on 31 August, 1912, and, with that phase completed, he joined the old cruiser HMS *Onyx* serving as a submarine depot ship at Devonport. His first submarine was the *A7*, where he served first under Geoffrey Warburton and then Philip Phillips. Both were to prove successful wartime commanding officers and we can be sure that young Hallifax had to serve a tough apprenticeship to satisfy these two demanding officers.

There Hallifax remained until leaving to join the new *E7* still building in Chatham. Here the tall, keen, smart young man, experienced only in the old A class but having served a tough apprenticeship under determined commanding officers, was to meet Feilmann. Feilmann, a much shorter man, took a more lighthearted view of life but was nevertheless an experienced commanding officer. These were the two who were to take the new submarine to sea, with war even then was looming on the horizon.

TABLE I: EARLY SUBMARINE CHARACTERISTICS

	FRENCH *Narval*	HMS *Holland 1*	HMS *A1*	GERMAN *U1*
Completed	1899	1903 (Completed after *No 2*)	1903	1907
Length	111ft 6ins	63ft 10ins	103ft 3ins	138ft 9ins
Beam	12ft	11ft 9ins	11ft 10ins	11ft 10ins
Surface Displacement	117 tons	105 tons	190 tons	238 tons
Dived Displacement	202 tons	120 tons	204 tons	283 tons
Torpedo Tubes	No Tubes 4 External torpedoes	1 × 18ins	1 × 18ins	1 × 18ins
Surface Speed	9.8 knots	7.4 knots	9.5 knots	10.8 knots
Dived Speed	5.3 knots	6.0 knots	6.0 knots	8.7 knots
Surface Endurance	345 miles at 8.5 knots	235 miles	235 miles	1500 miles at 10.0 knots
Dived Endurance	58 miles at 3 knots	20 miles at 5.0 knots	20 miles at 5.0 knots	25 miles at 5.0 knots
Crew	12	8	11	12

2

Countdown To War

ON 28 JUNE, 1914, a group of Serbian extremists in Sarajevo murdered an Austrian Archduke, the heir to the throne of the Austro-Hungarian Empire, and his wife and thereby set Europe on an irrevocable course to war. Yet, despite the fact that the peace of Europe had been almost constantly under one threat or another since the turn of the century, this latest crisis occurred at a time when the continent was outwardly calm, and few saw the effects of this act.

Until the late 1890s the German Navy was a coastal defence force committed to do little more than protect the Baltic shores of the fatherland. Two Naval Laws in 1898 and 1900 allowed for a massive increase in the size of the German Navy and was aimed at challenging the power of the Royal Navy which had confidently ruled the waves for the past century, secure in the knowledge of its success at Trafalgar.

Naturally there was concern about this expansion of naval power by Germany at a time when Britain had no formal alliance with any other major European power. On 15 November, 1901, Lord Selborne, then First Lord of the Admiralty, circulated a memorandum to the Cabinet which read, in part:

The Naval policy of Germany is definite and persistent. The Emperor seems determined that the power of Germany shall be used all the world over to push German commerce, possessions and interests.

Although King Edward VII carried out a state visit to Germany for the Kiel Regatta in June, 1904, and was accompanied by some units of the Fleet, both sides continued to view each other with suspicion and mistrust, and new ships for the fleets were being built at the limit of each nation's industrial capacity. Jingoistic remarks by Admiral Lord Fisher, and others, were widely reported and distorted to add fuel to the fires of suspicion. German moves in Morocco in 1905 and again in 1911 increased the tempo of what had become an armaments race which was not alleviated by the International Conference at the Hague in 1907. After the Agadir crisis in 1911 the Germans for their part felt frustrated, believing that but for Britain's unwarranted interference in what was essentially a Franco-German dispute they would have obtained a more favourable settlement. They drew the moral that a bigger fleet was essential if the Fatherland was not to be outmanoeuvred again.

Italy and Turkey went to war in 1911 over Italy's claim for colonial expansion in North Africa, the fighting carrying over into the following year. Taking advantage of Turkey's preoccupation with Italy, a league of Balkan States attacked her in the autumn of 1912, leaving the victorious allied armies almost at the gates of Constantinople before peace was signed in May, 1913. Later in 1913 war broke out again in the Balkans when the victors fell out among themselves and attacked the Bulgars, allowing the Turks to step in and recover some of their lost territory.

It is of interest that during this war a submarine made the first ever torpedo attack on an enemy ship. At 8.30 am on 9 December, 1912, the new Greek submarine *Delphin*, based on the recently captured island of Tenedos – a place to be met with again in this story – sighted the Turkish cruiser *Medjidieh* and five destroyers leaving the Dardanelles. An hour later he fired a torpedo at a range of only 500 yards. It failed to function and so Lieutenant Paparrigopoulos and his crew not only made the first torpedo attack but were also the first to suffer the frustrations and disappointments of a miss.

By the summer of 1914 the attention of British politicians was focused not across the North Sea on Germany but, rather, westward towards Ireland. The Government decision to give Home Rule to Ireland brought threats of Civil War. Rival factions armed themselves and made ready. Troops were sent to prevent bloodshed and to ensure that the plan was carried out, but this led to worse trouble, with many of the officers threatening to resign rather than be in a position to order troops to enforce the Home Rule Bill.

This was the Europe whose façade of peace was broken by the assassins of Sarajevo. Even the British and German navies were making a show of friendship at the annual Kiel Regatta with the British specially invited for the occasion, which was also to mark the re-opening of the Kiel Canal. As part of the German naval construction programme, the canal had been closed for widening and deepening to take all the new, larger battleships.

Four of Britain's latest battleships and three light cruisers joined the might of the German navy to watch the Kaiser perform the ceremony. This was followed by the usual round of official calls, visits, dances and sailing races. But events in far-off Sarajevo brought the proceedings to an abrupt end as the German Court went into official mourning for the Austrian couple. As the two fleets parted company most officers, both British and German, regarded the assassinations as just another Balkan incident soon to be forgotten; few saw that this was to be the fuse for the war regarded by the likes of Winston Churchill and Admiral Fisher as inevitable. And so it seemed, for while the Austrian Government considered what steps they should take and gauged what support they would have from their ally Germany, the situation remained calm. The German High Seas Fleet even sailed on 10 July to begin exercises in the Skagerrak before continuing northwards to Norway where it split into smaller groups to make preplanned visits to various ports.

The British, by coincidence and unknowingly, were following a much more realistic course for the crisis which had yet to develop. The summer naval manoeuvres of 1913 had had the object of testing the possibilities of enemy troops being landed on British soil. The attacking fleet had succeeded all too well and their submarines had inflicted significant damage on the defenders. Both the First Lord of the Admiralty, Mr Winston Churchill, and the First Sea Lord, Prince Louis of Battenburg, were convinced that a repeat of these manoeuvres in 1914 would not be necessary and instead had decided to conduct a test mobilization, with a naval review by the King followed by a short combined fleet exercise. In all it would be a much cheaper scheme than six weeks' exercises by the fleet, a move welcomed by the Liberal Government of Mr Asquith after years of massive expenditure on new construction for the Navy.

Orders for mobilization were issued on 10 July and, although some difficulties were experienced as there was no actual emergency and the

Reservists could not be compelled to report for duty, the vast majority of them did so. Some 20,000 men, Reservists and Pensioners, reported to their depots over the next few days and enabled all the ships scheduled for service in the War Plan to be made ready for service. In this way, with crews brought up to strength, the ships of the Second and Third Fleets joined those of the First Fleet for an impressive Naval Review at Spithead. When assembled, the three fleets – the First consisting of the normally fully operational ships, the Second of those ships in reserve but with normally reduced complements of officers and ratings, while the Third was of the oldest ships with crews made up entirely of those specially mobilized – made up most of the established strength of the Royal Navy with very few ships absent either on duty or abroad. As part of the exercise all the training establishments were closed and the men sent off to join their ships. Every effort was made to make the test as realistic as possible.

Anchored in the Solent with this impressive armada of surface ships were some of the submarines, including Feilmann's *E7*, described by *The Times* as "looking pert and pugnacious while offering a striking contrast between the old and new navy". But above all Saturday the 25th was a day of the traditional naval pageantry, beginning at 8 o'clock when the ships anchored in eleven long lines stretching through the Solent as far as the eye could see, all dressed with masthead ensigns at a signal from the old flagship HMS *Victory*, then still afloat in the harbour abeam of the dockyard. Portsmouth and Gosport were *en fête* and numbers of small craft crowded with gaily dressed visitors put out from the shore to see the sights.

For the King the weekend with his Fleet had been curtailed not by the looming crisis in Europe but by the one across the Irish Sea, and he was unable to arrive in Portsmouth before 5 pm. A gun salute from the Fleet to acknowledge his arrival coincided with the arrival overhead of some of the new aircraft of the Royal Naval Air Service. After sunset a rocket soared into the air from the flagship HMS *Iron Duke* and the Solent became ablaze with thousands of twinkling lights of the illuminations of the ships. Later still the crowds were thrilled by the massive searchlights of the battleships throwing their beams into the air and across the Solent.

Sunday the King spent informally with his Fleet. As the Royal Yacht *Alexandra* flying the Royal Standard sailed out of Portsmouth harbour and passed the grey stone walls of Fort Blockhouse, where the submariners were making their main base, there was only the strident note of the bugle calling ships' companies to attention; no guards, no bands or gun salutes, no formal manning of the ships' sides. In the course of the day His Majesty managed to visit a representative number of ships of the assembled fleet.

The following day the ships steamed past, with the King now on board the larger yacht *Victoria and Albert*. At 15 knots the massive fleet, including twenty-four dreadnoughts and thirty-five predreadnoughts, took six hours to pass. Noticeably there the odd puff of black smoke from the funnels of some of the ships of the Second and Third Fleets as their out-of-practice stokers and engineers strove to recapture lost skills. The King returned to London while the ships were conducting exercises for the next few days before the recalled men were due to disperse again.

Meanwhile events in the Balkans had remained relatively calm since the murders in Sarajevo. The Austrians had sent a high-ranking member of the Foreign Ministry, Herr Freidrich Wiesner, to the city to attempt to find out whether the Serbian Government was involved in any way with events. It was not an easy task, especially considering the emotive nature of the investigation as viewed from Vienna. Yet on 13 July he was able to report:

> There is nothing to show the complicity of the Serbian Government in the direction of the assassination, or in its preparations, or in the supplying of weapons. Nor is there anything to lead one to conjecture such a thing; on the contrary, there is evidence to show that complicity is out of the question.

Even the Germans came to similar conclusions as recorded by the former Chancellor von Bülow in his *Memoirs:*

> Although the horrible murder was the work of a Serbian Secret Society with branches all over the country, many details prove that the Serbian Government had neither instigated nor desired it. The Serbs were exhausted by two wars and even the most hot-headed must have paused at the thought of war with Austria-Hungary, so overwhelmingly superior. In Serbia's rear were the rancorous Bulgars and the untrustworthy Roumanians.

Weisner's was not a view which was received with satisfaction in Vienna where almost any incident would have sufficed to spark off a row with Serbia. Perhaps it is surprising that it took so long for the crisis to develop, for it was the 23rd, a month after the assassination, when Vienna issued its harsh ultimatum to Belgrade. Its terms were such that no self-respecting country could accept, for to do so would mean the virtual end of the country's independence.

On the same day Admiral Callaghan proceeded to Weymouth Bay with the ships of the First Fleet, while the Second and Third Fleet ships returned to their base ports where the reservists and pensioners were to disembark on the 25th at the end of their period of recall and where the first watch of active service ratings were to go on post-manoeuvres leave. The *E7* and the other submarines were not present when the fleets steamed out for their exercises in the Channel but returned quietly to their base in Gosport. On the Tuesday the *E7*, with *E4* and *E6*, went out and fired practice torpedoes at an old torpedo boat. Leave for the first watch of submarine crews was not due to start until the following Monday but it is probable that Hallifax was allowed to go early as the submarine was due to go across to dock in Portsmouth that day to have fittings for the new wireless masts and repairs to some machinery items carried out.

From Weymouth the First Fleet was due to sail on the Monday (27th) to carry out a series of training exercises around the coast. But on the Sunday it became known that Serbia was mobilizing and that Vienna had ordered a partial mobilization of her armed forces. At 4 o'clock on that Sunday afternoon, with the First Lord away in Norfolk with Mrs Churchill who was unwell, Prince Louis issued orders that no ships of the First Fleet were to leave Portland until further orders, but were to carry out their exercise programme in that area. It was a decision with which the First Lord was in total agreement when he returned to London. The following day all further leave was cancelled and preparations were begun to bring all Second Fleet ships back to full complement and to complete with stores, fuel and ammunition.

On Russia's advice Serbia had sent a conciliatory note in reply to the Austrian ultimatum, while not acceding to all its demands. Nevertheless on 28 July Austria-Hungary declared war on Serbia and Germany rejected British proposals for an International Conference to settle the issue between the two now-warring nations. At 5 o'clock that evening the Admiralty took the step of ordering the Grand Fleet, as it was now to be known, to leave the next day for its war station at Scapa Flow, under the temporary command of the Vice-Admiral commanding the 2nd Battle Squadron, while the Commander-in-Chief himself went to the Admiralty to discuss future plans and operations in the now likely event of war. Because of the seriousness of the situation the fleet was to proceed through the Strait of Dover and up the East Coast to its war base. Before the fleet had even left the Channel the Austrians were bombarding Belgrade, the Russians were making preparations to support their fellow Slavs, while the Germans threatened mobilization unless these preparations ceased.

What of Keyes and the submarine flotilla? On his own initiative on the morning of Monday the 27th Keyes instructed that no leave was to be granted until further notice and then went up to the Admiralty to see the Chief of the War Staff. During these talks he was able to assure him that the submarines were ready for war and urge that they should be moved instantly to the North Sea and that the Dover flotilla should take up its station. Orders to this effect were issued by the Admiralty that evening. Meanwhile, the *E7* had moved into the Dockyard as planned, so that, when the *Maidstone* sailed with the rest of the submarines, she was left behind and did not sail until early on the Tuesday afternoon.

Keyes was again ordered to the Admiralty on the Wednesday where he met Admiral Callaghan, under whose orders the Eighth (Overseas) Flotilla was to operate in the event of war. While he was in London he found out that the submarines had been sent to a War Station on the Humber instead of at Harwich as he had expected. The War Orders had only recently been amended and rewritten and now contained this unexpected instruction. It is difficult to discover now just how this came about, whether as a planned change of base or merely as an administrative error. At Harwich the submarines would be close to the destroyer force with whom they were expected to operate. In any case Immingham on the Humber was totally unsuitable for it had a large rise and fall of tide which made it impossible to enter the small basin except during short periods either side of high water. Additionally, it would have been all too easy for the only submarines that the Royal Navy possessed which were capable of taking offensive action to have been cooped up in this tiny port by German minelaying. Needless to say, Keyes pressed for a change in this deployment and orders were issued that night for the flotilla to sail as soon as practicable for Harwich.

Hallifax, who had started his leave before Keyes' orders stopping leave for the flotilla were issued, had to be recalled. It is at this stage that he started keeping his diary, against all instructions, but it is against his writings that events of those days may now be viewed.

Wednesday 29 July
Yesterday while on leave at Chester received a telegram ordering me to rejoin at Immingham the following afternoon. HMS MAIDSTONE arrived there with eight other submarines of the flotilla at 6.0 pm and the submarines entered the lock and passed into the Basin. At 8.0 pm the MAIDSTONE came alongside the pier outside the lock and I went aboard to find that the E7 was then arriving; she had gone into the Dockyard at Portsmouth on Monday afternoon to have new shafts fitted to the capstan gear and had not been able to come out until 1.0 pm on Tuesday after the MAIDSTONE had sailed with the other boats. She came alongside and I went onboard. King [another submarine officer] had been lent to her in my absence, and had orders to return to Portsmouth on arrival at Immingham.

We entered the lock at about 9 o'clock and passed into the Basin astern of the MAIDSTONE and made fast alongside her. Found when I got to my cabin that my uniform which I had sent to London to be cleaned before I went on leave had not been returned and all I had to wear was one new monkey jacket, one filthy and torn sea-going jacket and similar trousers.

The other boats had completed with torpedoes and war stores during Monday night. We spent until 3.0 am hoisting in four spare torpedoes, eight warheads – four of which we fitted – and the remainder of our war stores. Completed with fuel and lubricating oil and got a charge for the batteries from the MAIDSTONE. Slept in the boat.

Thursday 30 July
At 7.0 am I had just succeeded in collaring a bathroom when a voice outside shouted "All submarine officers down in your boats and stand by to shove off." So I only had time for a quick splash and then back to the boat where I found that we were to proceed to Harwich. We entered the lock with the other boats and at 9.0 am were let out into the river, where we lay until the MAIDSTONE came out. HMS ADAMANT which had arrived with the E7 the night before and had anchored in the river overnight was then ordered to weigh and proceed with the E3, E7 and E8. After lunch we were signalled by the ADAMANT to proceed at 13 knots to a position north-west of the Haisboro Lightship where we were to attack the MAIDSTONE as she went by, no torpedoes were to be fired. We got a very warm shaft bearing forward of the clutch and had to slow down but still arrived in position in plenty of time. It was very difficult to

catch a trim with all the fuel, stores and spare torpedoes onboard and we were very heavy aft. Made a successful attack and then rose [surfaced] and got under way, steering to rejoin the other two boats. We took station astern of the E8 with the E3 in sight some miles astern and the MAIDSTONE and ADAMANT with the remainder of the flotilla about five miles ahead steering for Yarmouth Roads. We soon lost sight of the E3 but the ADAMANT signalled that we would be exercising with her the next day and the submarines would anchor for the night behind Bawdsey Bank. Worked on the torpedoes all day, charging them with air and fitting sinking valves etc. They were all ready except for the firing pistols by midnight at which time we anchored in company with the E8 and to starboard of the MAIDSTONE.

Friday 31 July
At 5.0 am the MAIDSTONE weighed with the other submarines, having sent over two collision heads before she went, indicating that we were to fire torpedoes during our attacks and making every one fed up at the thought of all the wasted work last evening. In fact we were ordered to prepare two torpedoes to fire in two attacks. At 7.30 we sailed with the ADAMANT and the E3 who had arrived during the night, having been delayed for four hours as a result of an engine filling up with water. The E3 got permission to go straight to Harwich leaving us and the E8 to carry out our attacks between the SUNK and the SHIPWASH Lightships. We dived at noon and had a long attack to make as the ADAMANT approached round the banks and was in sight for a long time. On completion the E8 asked permission to return to harbour and make good a defect and we hoped to be excused our second attack, but no. It was a farcical attack, wasting battery power and fuel and the men's strength for they were pretty well tired out after four nights' and days' hard work.

We then went to Harwich and alongside the MAIDSTONE to complete with fuel, fresh water, stores and emergency provisions.

It is difficult to see what was achieved by all this exercising; Keyes wanted to get his valuable depot ships to Harwich where they would not be bottled up as in Immingham and not caught at sea in case of a sudden outbreak of war, yet they spent two days doing what could have been done in one. There was also the waste of effort caused by the absence of any forethought about what was wanted and one can sympathize with the sense of frustration that begins to show in Hallifax's diary.

We had received no news since Wednesday night and were glad to get the papers. The Examination Service★ was in force outside Harwich which showed us that things were not peaceful. Russia was still mobilizing apparently, but there was no other news.

The D7 has joined the flotilla, and several extra officers – all the submarine training class – have arrived and have been distributed among the senior boats as Third Officers. We do not get one being one of the junior boats.

However, Hallifax need not have worried, for within days Lieutenant Robinson joined the E7 as an additional watchkeeper. Robinson had been in the same term as Hallifax in the *Britannia* and by August, 1914, had started on a training course learning to be a specialist Gunnery Officer rather than a submariner. When all training had been halted he had been sent to the *Maidstone*. He left again to resume his specialist training on 14 August and the following day Sub-Lieutenant Anthony Cunard arrived to take his place. Cunard, too, was already known to Hallifax for he had been serving in the battleship *St Vincent* when Cunard had joined as a new midshipman. Now, with no previous submarine training or experience, he was to learn his trade at sea in the *E7*.

Events now moved rapidly. On 30 July the King was constrained to write in his diary "Foreign telegrams coming in all day, we are doing all we can for peace and to prevent a European war but things look very black . . . The debate in the House of Commons on the Irish question today had been postponed on account of the situation." The following day, when the Grand Fleet, as the First Fleet was now known, arrived at Scapa the Stock Exchange was closed and the Bank Rate was doubled to 8 per cent. While the fleet had been steaming majestically northwards to Scapa Flow so the German High Seas Fleet returned to Germany after its visit to Norway. By the 30th the Kaiser had been persuaded to order cautionary war measures for the fleet, though their main concern at that time was Russia and it was still hoped that Britain would not become involved in any conflict. Even so, the following day the more modern units of the fleet moved through the Kiel Canal to North Sea ports, leaving only the older ships to face the Russians. More ominously, German yachts withdrew from the regatta at Cowes, yet with an unusually warm summer most Britons remained unaware of the rapidly developing crisis and were preoccupied with arrangements for the forthcoming Bank Holiday.

★ Small cutters used to check the papers of incoming merchant ships.

Others were even setting off to spend August in the smart continental resorts.

Saturday 1 August

The 3rd Destroyer Flotilla were at buoys abreast of us and all day they were landing cabin furniture which looks like business. The 1st Flotilla have been doing the same thing higher up the Stour. Commodore (S) was flying his pendant in the MAIDSTONE and this pleased us as we felt we should get plenty of news.

No war news in the papers beyond the report of the Austrians bombarding Belgrade, but the evening papers say that the Germans have sent an ultimatum to Russia requiring her to stop mobilizing. In the evening we heard that Germany had declared war on her. Now we are bound to come into this arena, I fancy, as France must assist Russia and we shall assist France.

Sunday 2 August

The papers carry the news of the declaration of war on Russia by Germany and the intention of Italy to remain neutral. "The Observer" in a very fine article tells us there is a difference of opinion in the Cabinet over the question of our duty to France. It is inconceivable that the present Government, even, could back out and leave France to be knocked out even if there is no obligation to assist her should she declare war on Germany. Yet we have an obligation to Luxembourg whose neutrality we guaranteed and that has been violated by Germany, or so it is rumoured. Apart from obligations there is our own safety and future to consider should France be defeated and should the Germans seize ports in Belgium, Denmark and Holland.

After dinner the Captains of the submarines were ordered to open certain secret orders which contained code for use with the French Fleet – great excitement! Previous to this we heard that we had informed Germany that we should not permit her ships to pass into the North Sea or Straits of Dover to attack the French ports.

Monday 3 August

"The Times" announced that decisions of the first importance would be announced in the House of Commons this afternoon. It also printed a very clear article showing the issues at stake. During the forenoon we thought everything would be all right, but after lunch Feilmann told me that the Commodore had been speaking to him and confirmed the report of the split in the Cabinet. As the afternoon wore on and no orders came we got more and more alarmed. The sole topic of conversation was the question of whether the Government could possibly back out of assisting France, in which case the honour of England would be lost for ever, for no nation would ever again trust a Power who would back out at the moment of danger or even delayed in coming forward to assist.

Already it is 24 hours since Luxembourg's neutrality was violated and 12 since the Germans set foot in Belgium. Whether or not France has yet gone to war with Germany we cannot quite make out.

We have been informed by the Admiralty that Germany is sowing mines round Cuxhaven, Heligoland and all that coast and we are sitting in harbour and allowing them to do it.

We were mad with rage and vowing that if we failed to act we should resign when everything had settled down and then go abroad. Why, never again would an English Fleet dare visit a foreign port, for instead of being received as we were accustomed we should probably be spat on, or not allowed to visit. Remaining neutral would mean the gradual downfall of the Empire for trade would go with our credit and the Colonies would probably prefer to cut adrift from such a country.

The 6 o'clock paper depressed us still more, though we tried to find comfort without success in the thought that there must be some good reason for delay, but it would have to be a mighty good reason to allay the distrust which must have already been created in France.

At 7.45 pm another edition carried the news of Sir Edward Grey's announcement in the House of Commons. It was not very clear and seemed to imply that we were going to leave the French in the lurch. The only clear sentence was "If the Germans attack French ports, for my part, I consider it our duty to assist the French." That evidently meant that others were not of the same way of thinking. Dinner was the gloomiest meal I have ever attended, there was not a smile but plenty of bitter curses.

During dinner the Commodore returned from the Admiralty and the Secretary, who had been sitting next to me, went up to receive him. When he returned he told us that Keyes was spluttering with rage and had said that in London he had heard that the French Ambassador had called on Sir Edward Grey and asked him "Is there no such word as Honour in the English language?" That was the last straw dispelling any hopes that there was a good reason for our delay. To think that for the last six years during which the Navy has had to live almost at war pressure with the idea of defeating Germany when she should give us the chance of it, or at any rate of upholding the British Empire, and then to find our efforts have been wasted as when the hour came we had shown the White Feather, or rather the Government had and they are supposed to represent the Nation.

We tried to turn in and wait for the next morning's papers but kept returning to the smoking room to see if there might be any further news. Our one hope when we finally turned in about midnight was that the

Nation would insist on our honour being preserved, and we looked forward to reading the papers.

Tuesday 4 August.

I think that everyone was on deck at 7.30 waiting for the papers to come off and when the boat eventually came alongside we made a rush at the man. We tore them open and to our amazement saw such headlines as "Sir E Grey's Great Speech", or "Parliament Rises To The Occasion" etc. I read right through Sir Edward's speech, and it was a great one. That rotten evening paper had tried to condense it and done this so badly as to give the wrong idea!

I, and I think most of my fellow officers, if not all, do not want war for the sake of war and fighting. It will be very interesting to see whether all our strenuous training has been on the right lines, to see the value of submarines in actual warfare, and if the war has to come soon I am glad to be in it, but apart from that I have no wish to fight for the sake of fighting for it will be a ghastly affair under modern conditions. I think that we in submarines have every chance of being killed and I am not anxious for that, but when it comes to a question of England's honour there is only one feeling about it. I am very glad of that mistake yesterday for it showed that feeling very strongly.

During the afternoon we heard that the Government had sent an ultimatum to Germany requiring the strict observance of the neutrality of Belgium. This ultimatum expires at midnight.

I went ashore and walked to Dovercourt after tea. The place was full of soldiers, regulars and territorials, and there were soldiers guarding the pier. Got hold of my uniform at the station and had no further reason to wait for war!

In the evening paper I read that Germany's reply had been unsatisfactory. Going down to the pier at 7 o'clock I found boats from the AMPHION bringing officers' gear ashore. All ships in harbour were preparing for battle. Going onboard again I heard that war was to be declared at midnight.

After dinner the Commodore spoke to the crews of the submarines who were mustered on the quarterdeck. I could not get up the hatch for some time owing to the crush so missed the first sentences, but they explained the cause of the war. I got up to hear him say "Now don't imagine we are going to war just to help Serbia, it is nothing to do with that. Germany used Serbia as a tool to bring it about and it is such a dastardly outrageous thing that I don't believe God could let her come victorious out of this. You must go into this seeing red and that's the only way". He paused and was just going on again when a voice sung out "We'll give it to 'em, Sir, don't you worry about it" and there was a great roar from us all. Half a dozen men started half a dozen different tunes and just as "Rule Britannia" was about to win the Commodore said "That will do – better keep that for the end." He then wished us luck and goodnight.

During these first days days of August, 1914, events had moved steadily towards a general European War and despite Hallifax's doubts recorded at length in his diary it was not so much a case of if Great Britain would go to war but when. On the evening of the 31st the British Ambassador in Berlin had told the Germans that Britain would not countenance any violation of Belgian neutrality. At about the same time the Germans issued an ultimatum to the Russians demanding a cessation of warlike preparations within twelve hours. The following day Sir Edward Grey saw the German Ambassador in London to warn him again that any violation of Belgian neutrality might force Britain to take action. In the afternoon it was learnt that the Germans were holding up British shipping from leaving German waters.

At 7.30 pm (British time) on the 1st the German Ambassador in St Petersburg handed the formal declaration of war to the Russians, the news of this being carried by Reuters to the Admiralty in London where they learnt of this latest move in some three hours. The following day the Government gave the French an assurance which was in accordance with previous undertakings that if the German Fleet came through the North Sea or into the Channel to undertake hostile operations against the French then the British Fleet would also become involved.

As a counter to this undertaking to the French the Germans, for their part, tried to bid for British neutrality with their own promise that the High Seas Fleet would not approach the English Channel or the north coast of France. Yet they would not go as far as to give any assurance as to the fate of Belgium and that was crucial to British thinking. On the 3rd Germany declared war on France at 6.0 pm, while at the same time they tried to persuade the Belgians to allow them free movement of their troops through their country. The Belgians neither would, nor could, agree and their fate was sealed.

The final stage began on the 4th with the news that the Germans had actually moved their armies into Belgium. A British ultimatum, to expire at midnight, was immediately sent to Berlin demanding the withdrawal of all troops. There was no reply. At 11.0 pm (i.e. at midnight German time) Mr Churchill authorized the Admiralty to send the war telegram to all naval ships and establishments and we were at war. In fact it was an academic move by then for at 6.30 pm in Berlin the Germans declared war on Britain, a move that was unknown to the Foreign Office in London for some hours.

Despite the long build-up to the almost inevitable declaration of war, neither Fleet was really deployed for instant offensive action. Both sides were at their War Stations and ready to meet any attack which might be made on their coasts. In days when the use of radio was rather uncertain it is perhaps possible that ships deployed offensively might not have received the right orders and both Admiraltys wished to keep control of their forces.

Hallifax's attitude to the approaching war may sound quaint to today's public, but in 1914 it was not untypical. In London and elsewhere the outbreak of war was greeted with wild acclaim and cheering crowds outside Buckingham Palace where the King and Queen made a brief appearance on the balcony. The following day thousands of young men rushed to enlist. The mood in London was matched in Berlin. Both countries felt that they were going to war to honour their obligations to an ally. In Britain there was an added sense of obligation to both Belgium and Luxembourg. In Germany they still remembered the heady days of 1870–71 and perhaps sensed another easy victory over the French.

Showing clearly through this account of the final days of peace is the dependence of the public on the newspapers and the effects of rumours and speculation; no radio or instant TV coverage for this crisis. Huge crowds waited around for news. On the days immediately before the die was cast people surged along Whitehall and then waited for hours near Downing Street to hear the rumours or to try and gauge what the Government would do next. Traffic was reduced to chaos, work was neglected in the anxiety to hear the news. While the feeling of the vast majority of the nation was almost solidly pro-war, Keir Hardie, the pioneer Labour M.P., presided over a peace rally in Trafalgar Square.

Despite the public fervour, Mr Asquith presided over a divided Cabinet. The Foreign Minister, Sir Edward Grey, made superhuman efforts to achieve a non-military settlement, but came to realize the inevitable. One of those strongly against the war was the Chancellor of the Exchequer, Mr Lloyd George, who, ironically, was to become the Prime Minister who finally led the country to victory. On the other hand Mr Winston Churchill at the Admiralty saw that no other course was possible. The French suffered from no divisions, no wavering; the memory of 1871 was still strong and the sense of shame still hurt. Now was the chance for revenge.

3
Early Days

THE PRIMARY TASK of the Royal Navy in 1914 was to destroy the enemy's fleet and to seize and maintain command of the North Sea and Channel in order to prevent the enemy from making any serious attack on British territory or trade or interfering with the passage of the Expeditionary Force. The attainment of this was simplified by the relative geographical position of Britain and Germany. Command of the exits to the North Sea could be achieved from bases which were nearer for the British than for the Germans and ensured that the Germans would have to fight to deploy any major surface force against the trade routes or British overseas possessions. It also ensured the safety of the routes for the transports taking an army to France and at the same time cut off most of the flow of German maritime trade. Command of the North Sea was made easier for the Royal Navy by an agreement with the French which allowed the British to concentrate in home waters while the French fleet would dominate the Mediterranean.

The Germans hoped that British tactics would be to keep a close watch on their coast and the exit from the Baltic, and this was in fact to have been the case until only a few years before 1914. Had this been so the Germans hoped to provoke a series of comparatively minor actions in which they would have had local superiority and which would have been successfully concluded before the main British fleet could concentrate. By these actions the Germans hoped they would whittle away the overall superior strength of the Royal Navy which would finally leave them dominant. For their part the British, by carrying out a policy of distant blockade, forced the Germans to come to them if they desired a fleet action, a course which would always leave the Germans vulnerable, though as will be seen, not one which the British were necessarily able to exploit.

The German North Sea coast, bordering the Heligoland Bight on two sides, which was to feature so much in British submarine operations over the next four years, was only about 200 miles long between the Dutch and Danish borders. Four main rivers flowed north into the Heligoland Bight along the 70 miles of coast to the east of the Dutch border, and at their mouths lay the German fleet bases and anchorages. The easternmost river, the Elbe, is the gateway to the great port of Hamburg, and on it lies the smaller port of Brunsbüttel, which is the western end of the Kiel Canal. The next river to the west is the Weser with the ports of Bremen and Bremerhaven. Between the Elbe and the Weser is the low sandy peninsular with the port of Cuxhaven, while between Cuxhaven and Brunsbüttel lay the fleet anchorage off Altenbruch.

Further to the west again and flowing into the sea through the almost landlocked bay of the same name is the Jade. On the north side of Jade Bay lies the great naval base of Wilhelmshaven, where a bustling dockyard with docks, jetties, workshops and arsenal replaced a fishing village which existed before the expansion of the Imperial Navy. Despite being the entrance to the principal port for the German fleet, the river wound through sandbanks and required frequent dredging, even within the well-marked navigational channel, and the bar at the mouth of the river could not be crossed by the larger ships except at certain times around high water. Further out, the estuary widens to become the Schilling Roads which was habitually used as a fleet anchorage at times of readiness. The westernmost river is the Ems, actually forming the border with Holland for parts of its length, with the port of Emden at its mouth. In 1914 it was the base for only light craft and cruisers, though it was to become an important centre for U-boats in the years to come.

Lying a few miles offshore is a chain of seven main islands, the German Frisian Islands stretching from off Schilling Roads eastward for 50 miles, including Norderney and Borkum, the latter lying off the mouth of the Ems. These islands, with an intricate network of shallow channels and sandbanks which are only just covered at high tide, form an effective defensive chain off the coast. Out in the Bight, to the north of Cuxhaven, and heavily fortified in 1914, lies the island of

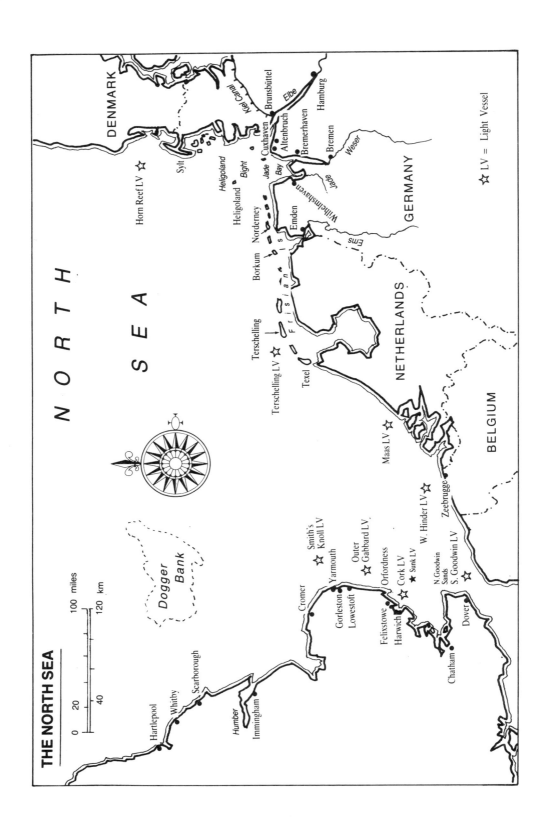

THE NORTH SEA

NORTH SEA

DENMARK

GERMANY

NETHERLANDS

BELGIUM

Dogger Bank

☆ LV = Light Vessel

Horn Reef LV ☆

Sylt

Heligoland

Heligoland Bight

Jade Bay

Brunsbüttel
Cuxhaven
Altenbruch
Bremerhaven
Hamburg
Bremen
Elbe
Kiel Canal
Weser
Jade
Wilhelmshaven
Emden
Norderney
Borkum
Ems

Terschelling
Terschelling LV ☆
Texel
Frisian Is.

Maas LV ☆

W. Hinder LV ☆
Zeebrugge

Smith's Knoll LV ☆
Yarmouth
Gorleston
Lowestoft
Cromer

Outer Gabbard LV ☆
Orfordness
Felixstowe
Harwich
Cork LV ☆
★ Sunk LV
N. Goodwin Sands
S. Goodwin LV ☆
Dover
Chatham

Hartlepool
Whitby
Scarborough
Humber
Immingham

100 miles
120 km
0 20 40

Heligoland. Its small harbour could accommodate light cruisers, destroyers and submarines, and became one of the first of the Imperial Navy's seaplane bases.

German defensive arrangements in the Heligoland Bight were designed to delay any attack on the German coast, giving enough warning for their fleet to get to sea. By day an outer line of destroyers patrolled across an arc 35 miles from the Elbe Lightship with small torpedo boats forming an inner line some 12 miles further back. Between these two lines up to seven submarines would be on patrol, with any British attack being drawn over them as the destroyers fell back. At night the destroyers were to fall back to the inner patrol line while the torpedo boats and submarines returned to harbour, many using the newly constructed facilities on adjacent Heligoland. The expected attacks by British submarines could only be frustrated by the destroyers zig-zagging in the area at high speed, keeping the submarines submerged and exhausting the batteries, for at that time there was no depth charge or other weapon with which to attack a dived submarine.

The Germans clearly planned to use their submarines defensively in conjunction with their patrol craft. The British too saw the role of the submarine as one of co-operation with the destroyers and patrol craft. At Harwich the boats of Keyes' "Overseas" flotilla were to work with the two destroyer flotillas of Commodore Tyrwhitt's force. Elsewhere around the coast the older submarines, along with the older destroyers and torpedo boats, were stationed to provide local defence. The wartime directive issued by the Commander-in-Chief to Keyes made it clear that his submarines were to operate offensively against the German Fleet and into the Heligoland Bight. At this time neither side envisaged the use of submarines as a means of waging war on the other's commerce. Indeed, when Fisher had suggested in a memorandum in 1913 that this might be an option for the Germans to take in the future, the whole idea was rejected out of hand by both Battenburg and Churchill. Keyes himself commented that "we all discarded this possible behaviour as impossible and unthinkable."

As soon as Keyes had arrived in Harwich with the *Maidstone,* the *Adamant* and the submarines, he made his plans for the initial operations to begin as soon as war was declared. Two boats were then to proceed towards the Heligoland Bight, being towed by destroyers as far as Terschelling. If they returned with a favourable report they would be relieved by two more, though even Keyes considered these patrols as little more than a hazardous and tentative experiment in view of the state of reliability of the submarines' engines and the expected strain on the crews. Hence they were to be towed across the North Sea.

4 August
E6 and E8 were detailed for what seems to be a good place, as being a likely spot to catch some of the Germans and are on their own there. The other boats are working with the destroyers. E7 was one of those held back in reserve to our disgust, but the Commodore pointed out that it is no good being impatient as there will be heaps of opportunities.

The scheme is his own, he having got a free hand from the Admiralty; he has two destroyers – FIREDRAKE and LURCHER – told off for him and he is evidently longing for a chance to get at the enemy.

Early on 5 August the *E6* (Lieutenant-Commander C. P. Talbot) in the tow of the *Amethyst* and the *E8* (Lieutenant-Commander F. H. H. Goodhart) in tow of the *Ariel* sailed from Harwich to carry out the first operational patrols by submarines of the Royal Navy. At 1 am the following morning, when some 30 miles NNE of the Terschelling lightship, the two boats slipped their tows and proceeded independently into the Bight. Their orders were to remain not more than three days, and unless they were likely to be able to carry out successful offensive operations they were to return after two days.

5 August
E6 and E8 shoved off at 3.30 am. I woke and opened my deadlight and scuttle – it being daylight – and saw the other boats preparing to go. I turned out to see them off and went on deck. They left too early to get a cheer, but one or two others were up to wave to them besides the Commodore and the Captain.

By 5.45 am on the 6th the *E6* was only 23 miles from Heligoland. The following morning she glimpsed a U-boat on the surface but there was no opportunity to attack either then or at any other time during the patrol. She returned to Yarmouth on the 8th for Talbot to report to Keyes by telephone. The *E8* similarly made for the area where the German patrol lines were believed to be and then returned to Yarmouth late on the 8th. Both submarines had sighted and been sighted by the many German trawlers in the area who then frustrated their every attempt to get further into the Bight. Many of the trawlers were believed to be fitted with radio and were capable of reporting the presence of the two British boats. One of these trawlers so constantly dogged the *E6*'s movements that the submarine was surfaced and the trawler ordered by International Code to hoist her colours which, of course, were German. She was then ordered to stop. The trawler initially obeyed, but then followed the *E6* as she made for Heligoland. It was a difficult situation for Talbot as he had no gun to force compliance with his orders and a torpedo would have been wasted running under such a small target.

Four other submarines were also sent out; the *E4* (Lieutenant-Commander E. W. Lier), the *E9* (Lieutenant-Commander M. Horton), the *D3* (Lieutenant-Commander E. C. Boyle) and the *D5* (Lieutenant-Commander G. Herbert). The submarines were given a patrol line running south-eastwards from the Outer Gabbard light vessel and their task was to prevent any passage of the enemy's torpedo boats and destroyers towards the Dover Straits, and in this they were to co-ordinate with a sweep northwards by the 1st and 3rd Destroyer Flotillas. The submarines returned to Harwich without loss or incident but the destroyer sweeps led to the first shots of the war at sea.

> Woke to hear cheering. Looking out I saw about 40 Boys on the fo'c'sle of the GANGES (we were lying abreast of her) cheering the destroyers of the Third Flotilla as they steamed out. I turned out and found our ship's company on the boat deck also cheering vigorously. The Third Flotilla were followed by the FEARLESS and the First Flotilla. The GANGES Boys cheered every one of the 38 ships but our crew gave up four from the end, so we all saluted the last two to make up for it.

Immediately after the German declaration of war against England Korvettenkapitän Biermann, in command of the auxiliary cruiser *Konigin Luise*, was ordered to sail to lay his mines off the English coast. The ship was a converted ferry of some 1,800 tons normally employed on the Heligoland-Hamburg run. The short time allowed in Cuxhaven for her conversion to a minelayer allowed for little more than the installation of the mining gear, loading 180 mines and repainting the ship in the colours of the Great Eastern Railway Company whose own ferries ran from Harwich to the Hook of Holland. Two 88mm guns which were to have been fitted had to be left behind, though she did have two 37mm machine guns and some rifles. From the mouth of the River Ems the *Konigin Luise* went down the Dutch coast until west of the Maas light vessel at 7 am on the 5th when she altered course for the English coast. Often hidden by unseasonable rain squalls, there was hope that the minelay could be completed successfully and she could escape back to Germany using neutral Dutch waters. But it was not to be. Two destroyers, the *Lance* and *Landrail*, had been sent on ahead of the rest of their flotilla led by *HMS Amphion* to search for a merchant ship which had been reported by a passing trawler as acting suspiciously and throwing things overboard. Almost immediately the two warships sighed the *Konigin Luise* who turned away to try to complete her minelaying task and escape. After some initial bad shooting from the two destroyers and with some help from the *Amphion* the German ship was soon badly hit, on fire and sinking. By 11 am the first action of the war was over and the *Konigin Luise* had sunk, while the three British ships picked up the survivors, five officers and seventy men.

> Rumours of actions were current all day, but after lunch it was piped that the AMPHION had reported that the Third Flotilla had sunk the KONIGIN LUISE, a minelayer, and had picked up the crew. She was uncomfortably close to this place and we were relieved to hear that she had been destroyed with a large number of her mines still onboard. First blood anyhow is a good thing.

Once the rescue had been completed, the *Amphion* and *Landrail* rejoined the rest of the flotilla and continued on towards Terschelling while the *Lance* returned to Harwich with a defective gun. At 9 pm that evening they reached the limits of their sweep and turned for home, aiming to pass well clear of the suspected German minefield. Unfortunately their navigation was in error and at 6.35 am the following day the *Amphion*, leading her flotilla, ran right into trouble as a mine exploded under the ship forward of the bridge. There were heavy casualties among the seamen whose messdecks were under the forecastle, and among the German prisoners who had been housed in a space in the bow only one survived. With the ship rapidly sinking and on fire Captain Fox ordered the ship to be abandoned. It was as well that he did for soon afterwards a second mine exploded under the magazine. Writing in the *Naval Review* in 1917 he described the scene:

1. Lieutenant Oswald Hallifax.

2. Lieutenant-Commander "Ferdie" Feilmann. The ribbon of the Royal Humane Society's Bronze Medal is shown on the right breast. Feilmann was awarded the medal as an 18-year-old Midshipman serving in HMS *Crescent* for saving the life of a sailor who had fallen into the St Lawrence River at Quebec.

3. Commander A. D. Cochrane, DSO, RN, MP.

4. HMS *Maidstone* with submarines alongside at Harwich.

5. Submarines *E4*, *E16* and *D3* alongside HMS *Maidstone* at Harwich. The guns fitted on the forecasing of each submarine are clearly visible.

6. HMS *E7* seen leaving Harwich for the Mediterranean. HMS *E16* in the background.

7. Lieutenant Hallifax and a lookout on the bridge. The absence of
    any protection and the nearness of the sea are very apparent.

The foremost half of the ship seemed to rise out of the water and break into a mass of flame and smoke, causing a great upheaval in the water and a terrific roar resembling a volcano; masses of material were thrown into the air to a great height, and I personally saw one of the 4-inch guns and a man turning head over heels about 150 feet up; this gun just missed falling on the LINNET, much to the relief of her CO, who saw it coming and thought his number was up.

The *Amphion* lost one officer and 131 ratings killed, while on board the *Lark* the sole German survivor from the *Amphion* was killed when a flying 4-inch shell exploded.

But the events of this initial sweep by the Third Flotilla were not yet over. Approaching Harwich, the destroyers met another ferry in the colours of the Great Eastern Railway Company, as had been the *Konigin Luise*, and flying a German ensign at the yardarm. Two destroyers raced forward and immediately opened fire, and it was lucky that again the opening shots were poorly ranged, for the ferry was the *St Petersburg* conveying the German Ambassador and his staff out of England to Holland and due to return again with the British Ambassador on his way home from Berlin. After the German flag had been rapidly hauled down the ferry went on her way unscathed but chastened. Earlier, Commodore Keyes had arranged with the ferry's Master that he would steer an intricate series of courses leaving Harwich as though he was taking his ship through the swept channel of a defensive minefield. It is reported that these manoeuvres did not go unnoticed by the German Naval Attaché.

6 August

During the forenoon we wiped over the terminals of the forward battery and discovered one cell very low in acid. We had to lift it and the next cell as well and by 12.45 pm had got that one back and the leaky cell was standing on the battery boards. I had just told the hands to go to dinner when I heard my name shouted down the conning tower and a voice asking if I was shoving off, as all the other boats were going and there was a German flotilla outside. I thought I was having my leg pulled, but with the news that Feilmann was onboard I realized it was OK. I turned round and saw the battery cell being rapidly replaced by the hands who had a moment before been very weary, whilst the torpedo-man was hauling the torpedo back to put the pistol in. Feilmann did not appear again and I feared we were not going. I dashed inboard to find him calmly eating his lunch, said I was ready but he put a damper on my ardour by saying three boats had gone and we should not. The crew were very disappointed. The Commodore had dashed out in LURCHER and got a cheer as she passed, as did our three boats. About an hour later they all returned and we found there had been a mistake. The local defence flotilla had reported firing off the Sunk lightship and had believed it to be the Germans.

While the *E6* and *E8* were the sole British submarines to be sailed towards the German coast the Germans planned an ambitious operation for their First Submarine Flotilla in the North Sea designed to seek out and attack the battleships of the Grand Fleet, which they thought would be at sea between Scotland and Norway. Ten submarines, the *U5*, the *U7–9* and the *U13–18*, sailed from Heligoland early on the 6th and, having reached a position roughly in the centre of the North Sea, were to move northwards seven miles apart for about 300 miles before returning to Heligoland. Only major units of the British fleet were to be attacked while on the outward leg. These boats, the oldest in the German submarine fleet, were the contempories of the British 'D' class. The Germans had doubts about their reliability for an extended operation such as this but they had been selected as they tended to have more experienced commanding officers than the newer boats. Another factor was that they were fitted with the Korting heavy oil engine which tended to betray their presence when running on the surface with columns of smoke by day and flame from the exhaust by night. The *U5* was forced to return just before midday when she developed engine trouble. The sweep was unproductive. The *U13* failed to return and to this day her fate remains a mystery. The *U15* was sighted by the cruiser *Birmingham* early on the morning of the 9th. The cruiser turned quickly and struck the submarine a glancing blow, causing her to lose trim so that her number could be clearly seen on the conning tower. Opening fire with all guns that would bear, the *Birmingham* turned again and rammed the German amidships, cutting her in half. The *U15* thus goes into history books as being the first submarine to be sunk in war.

Not unexpectedly there was a rash of sightings of enemy submarines or their periscopes in these early days of war. The battleship *Monarch*, carrying out gunnery practice to the north-east of the Orkneys, reported being fired at during the morning of the 8th, while about 100 miles away to the south-east the two battleships *Iron Duke* and *Dreadnought* both claimed to have sighted periscopes, while the *St Vincent* sighted yet another. It is possible that one or more of these may have been the ill-fated *U13*, but it is unlikely for the positions are well to the west of her planned track. Like the German sighting of a British periscope near Heligoland on the afternoon of the 4th, long before any British submarine was in that area, these sightings were probably the result of imaginations brought to fever pitch by the outbreak of war. Whatever the reason or reality of the sighting, they convinced Admiral Sir John Jellicoe, who had taken over command of the Grand Fleet just before the outbreak of war, that there was a real threat to his capital ships and this influenced his plans and movements not just for the next few days but for the remainder of his time in command.

The *E7* had a first taste of the boredom of war on the evening of the 6th when they were told to go out. At first both Feilmann and Hallifax thought, and hoped, that it was to relieve the *E6* in the Bight, but they soon found that they were to join the *E3* (Lieutenant-Commander G. Cholmely) and the *D2* (Lieutenant-Commander A. G. Jameson) off Felixstowe in case of an expected German attack. Having spent a quiet but cold night secured to buoys the three submarines returned alongside the *Maidstone* the next morning.

> There was a full moon and it was nearly as light as day, so an attack seemed unlikely, but we trimmed down a bit, got the spare torpedoes ready for reloading the tubes in case of necessity and put an armed sentry on the bridge with orders to rouse everyone should he hear firing. We should get plenty of warning from the fire of the forts.

With the outbreak of war the Cabinet decided that an Expeditionary Force of four infantry divisions and one cavalry division should be sent to France. Movement of the force was scheduled to begin on 9 August and be completed on the fifteenth day afterwards. Commodore Keyes had already sent two pairs of submarines to patrol in the southern North Sea and, with the imminent departure of the BEF for France, he decided to increase the number of submarines on patrol there, being sure that the German High Seas Fleet would not miss such an opportunity to cause damage to the British with an average of twenty-four transports all full of troops crossing to France each day. The existing patrol line was to be increased to ten boats and moved some 15 miles to the southward in two lines. Keyes himself, in the destroyer *Lurcher*, with other senior submarine officers also embarked in destroyers, were to be in the vicinity both to co-ordinate the patrols and to be able to pass new orders rapidly to the submarines. It must be remembered that the radios fitted in the submarines were not very powerful, while some, like the *E5*, had no radios and others like the *E7* had receivers but no transmitters.

Friday 7 August
Feilmann told me just before dinner that I was to see that the crew had provisions for at least a week as we were to go out tomorrow, but this was not to be spoken of. I merely told the crew that enquiries were being made as to the number of days' provisions onboard and that all boats were to keep at least seven days' worth. I believe that the Expeditionary Force is to sail on Sunday and we are to keep their route clear. The destroyer patrols have been called in so I expect they are coming in to rest and then also to go out to keep the route clear. It will be a fine bit of work if the BEF can get away on Sunday. We ought to have some fun out there.

Saturday
Got our written orders just before dinner showing the positions we shall take tomorrow morning. The Commodore is going to see the Captains of all boats. (Not 2nd in Commands as well, worse luck.)

After one day on this new patrol line Keyes proposed to shift his patrols still further southward to the line North Goodwin – Sandettie – Ruytingen to reduce the area covered by the submarines and increase the chances of sighting any enemy ships. However, the 'B' and 'C' class submarines from Dover were operating on a line from the South Goodwins to Calais and perhaps because of this his plan was not approved at first. On the evening of the 10th the Admiralty had a change of heart and Keyes' submarines were brought down to the proposed line practically at the mouth of the Dover Strait. A third line was formed by the six French submarines from Calais and stretched across the Strait nearly 15 miles south-westward of the British patrol, while other French submarines from Cherbourg patrolled between Cap de la Hague and Portland to the westward of the transport routes.

The orders for the submarines laid down their patrol positions and stated that the patrols were to be on the surface with each pair of submarines keeping about 1½ miles apart. At night the boats were to collect around specific fixed navigational marks. The *E7*, with the *E5* (Lieutenant-Commander C. Benning), were to patrol by day positions between the Fairy Bank and the West Hinder light vessel, with the *E3* to be close to the light vessel at night. Only at the approach of an enemy would the submarines dive to make their attacks. To a modern submariner this may sound a strange way to conduct a patrol but it must be remembered that accurate navigation in waters with strong tidal streams was not easy, as the *Amphion* had already found out, and that detection of the enemy rested solely on an efficient visual lookout being kept. It is worth noting too that the older 'B' and 'C' class submarines of the Dover patrol actually secured up to buoys to conduct their patrol and returned to harbour at night.

Sunday 9 August

We got on our station and dived to get a trim. We were only down 15 minutes and then blew [surfaced] and when I got on deck I saw the *E5* starting to the south-west and the LURCHER approaching us. When she came close she signalled us to proceed to close the Ruytingen lightship and there await further orders. She added that the patrol lines had been altered. We have been there ever since in the company of the *E3*, *E5* and *D3*. There are very strong tides and we have continuously to run to the SW on the engines.

(Later). At 6.30 pm the FIREDRAKE signalled the four boats to close and sent a boat to collect the Captains. The skipper returned after 30 minutes with orders for us to anchor for the night and not to challenge anyone, not to reply to a challenge, but to keep quiet and sink [dive] if approached.

10 August

Woke and heard that the anchor was to be weighed at full speed and that a destroyer was coming towards us. Found Feilmann on the bridge and was told we were going to our position as it was nearly daylight. A destroyer was approaching us but it was the FIREDRAKE though it could easily have been an enemy. She signalled that the Admiralty had not approved the new patrol lines and we were going to those of yesterday.

(Later). At 5.0 pm the FIREDRAKE closed us again and told us that the Admiralty had now consented to the change of patrol positions. Once again we closed the Ruytingen light ship and were to anchor for the night. After anchoring opened the hatches for a short while to ventilate the boat.

On the 12th the Admiralty ordered Keyes to withdraw half his flotilla to Harwich with two boats – the *E5* and *E7* – being sent to Yarmouth in case the Germans raided towards the Norfolk coast. Two days later the remaining boats were withdrawn from patrol. The initial crossing of the BEF was completed on the 23rd, and then for the next fifty-one months there was a continuous, almost uninterrupted two-way flow of transports across the Channel with reinforcements, wounded, stores and leave parties.

Thursday 11 August
[The *E7* had bottomed for the night instead of anchoring.] At 2.30 am got ready for blowing [surfacing] when I heard a propeller passing over us. We waited till it had faded away and then blew. It was pretty dark and we could not see much but picked out a destroyer a little way off and she was signalling to us. She gave us orders to proceed to Yarmouth with the *E5*. We passed safely through the channel which the minesweepers had swept off the coast by Orfordness and arrived off Gorleston at noon.

Based on an intelligence assessment of the High Seas Fleet's movements the Admiralty arranged for Jellicoe to take the Grand Fleet back into the North Sea and conduct a sweep to ensure that the Germans did not approach either the English coast or move southwards to threaten the movement of the BEF. While the Grand Fleet sailed south Tyrwhitt's destroyers, with some old cruisers of the *Bacchante* class in support, were to sail north up to a line N 30° W from Terschelling. Keyes was to send four submarines to patrol off the Ems and the Weser. The presence of the old cruisers was of some concern to the two Commodores who considered them a liability and too vulnerable should they meet the Germans when they might present them with an easy success; they were unworked-up since commissioning, obsolete, manned almost entirely by reservists and pensioners and their guns had not been fired in years. The four submarines to take part were the *E5* and *E7* from Yarmouth, and the *D2* and *D3* from Harwich.

The Grand Fleet found nothing and turned north again on the 16th, though the scouting cruisers appear to have only narrowly missed meeting the German cruisers. For their part the Germans had no idea that the British were at sea in strength, let alone that they had come as close to Germany as they did. Tyrwhitt's destroyers too found nothing to attack although remaining near Terschelling until noon on the 17th when they also returned for home. The submarines had no successes to report but they had a rather more exciting time before they withdrew, also on the 17th.

E5 parted her tow soon after we started and the DRUID with E7 eased down to about 4 knots until the FIREDRAKE took her in tow again. After a good two hours they caught us up but the speed was then only 7 knots instead of the planned 12 knots. It's very pleasant being towed, having nothing much to worry about. At 3.0 pm the E5's tow parted again. This time they gave up the attempt and E5 came on under her own power. Before slipping the tow the FIREDRAKE signalled to us our position adding "I wish you the best of luck and a good bag".

Jameson in the *D2* repeatedly tried to attack an armoured cruiser moored in the Ems but was constantly thwarted by shoals. The *D3*, also off the Ems, saw little of importance but was attacked by a destroyer shortly before leaving the area. The *E5* and the *E7* were sent to the Weser where, having been attacked himself by a destroyer during the morning of the 16th, Benning made the first attack by a British submarine at 1.0 pm that day. The single torpedo missed the destroyer it was aimed at. The next morning it was the turn of the *E5* to have a lucky escape when a periscope was sighted only 100 yards away on the beam and Benning claimed that a torpedo passed under the stern as he dived rapidly with a 10° bow-down angle!

D2 came into Harwich after us. She was nearly caught off the Ems – running on the surface on her engines when she saw a destroyer dashing at her down the glitter of the sun and by then only a few hundred yards off. She opened out to full speed on her engines and turned eight point [90°] to make shooting more difficult. She then dived in absolutely record time. The destroyer hung about over her for a bit, but was out of sight when she surfaced again. Another pretty close thing.

The *E7* spent a frustrating time trying to avoid the enemy's patrols. On the 16th they were forced to spend a, for then, unprecedented time dived of nearly thirteen hours. Frequent looks through the periscope gave Feilmann several sightings of the German patrols and while the *E7*'s battery became more and more exhausted they were never in a position to attack these elusive craft. Eventually they were forced to bottom and remain quiet until after dark.

Never have I known such a long day. Here we are after the longest day of my life sitting on the bottom at a depth of 90 feet off the German coast and praying that when we get up we shall be able to run for it unseen and charge the battery.

(Later). The time spent on the bottom was slow in passing; we would start reading books or examine the charts and then someone would say "about time" [to surface] "I suppose?" and we would find that only a few minuts had passed. The boat got clammy and chilly. No cooking had been allowed since breakfast and lights were cut to a minimum. Meals have been bread and cold meat for lunch, cake for tea, dinner being biscuits when we thought of it, but by then it was so fuggy one did not want to eat. When we did surface and the hatch was opened the air rushed out – the barometer showed nearly 32 inches – and the atmosphere in the boat was visible, it formed a blue mist.

After an equally frustrating time dived during the following morning they found they were able to surface in the afternoon with no patrols in sight. They sighted the *E5* in the distance and, joining her, the two submarines headed towards Lowestoft, where they were to report, before going back to Harwich. But it was not to be a passage without excitement.

At 4.30 am on the 18th the *E5* with the *E7* about two cables (400 yards) on her port beam were proceeding south-eastwards towards Lowestoft when a four-funnelled cruiser was sighted hull down to the south. An hour later, when the ships were well within visual signalling range of each other, Benning hoisted the flag signal for the challenge, believing the cruiser to be one of the *Argyll* class and wishing to identify himself as "friendly", though Cunard, who was on watch in the *E7*, felt that the approaching cruiser did not look "quite right" to be an *Argyll*. The challenge was up for some time – Hallifax says ten minutes – when the cruiser eventually replied with a salvo from her 105mm guns which fell too close to the two submarines for comfort. The cruiser was in fact the German *Strassburg*, one of three sent out by the Germans to raid the British patrols if they could be found. She had reached the southern limit of her sweep and had just turned to return home when the submarines had first sighted her. Needless to say the submarines both dived quickly and were very lucky to escape the many shells fired at them. To the chagrin and apparent fury of Hallifax they had not only missed the chance of attacking the German but had acted in a most un-professional manner. That an experienced commanding officer like Benning should have behaved in this way when they all believed that the correct doctrine was to dive instantly is not explained. Feilmann had not even gone to the bridge, but had passed the details of the recognition challenge and reply to Cunard and then turned in again.

That the two boats had had the goddess of fortune on their side was all too evident from the marks of splinters and ricochets that could be seen when they surfaced again.

Although the Admiralty sent a congratulatory signal to Keyes for the way that the submarines had acted in this operation, it was received without enthusiasm by the submarines' crews who realized how little had been achieved and what the cost might have been. Indeed it is difficult to see why the message was sent.

Submarines in those early days of the war had hardly covered themselves with glory, nor indeed had they shown that they were liable to capitalize on their potential; fears by both sides of their prowess had not been realized, though this was soon to come. At this stage the Germans were no better than the British and had lost two submarines in the course of events. Meanwhile, in the *E7* the tensions were beginning to show which, as will be seen, were to lead to a dramatic climax in the next few months.

4

Battles In The Bight

ON 23 AUGUST three submarines returned from patrol in the Heligoland Bight, delivered their reports to Keyes and set in train a series of events that was to lead to what became known as the Battle of the Heligoland Bight, the first major encounter of the war between the fleets of Britain and Germany, the fleets whose race for supremacy had played so large a part in Europe's slide into war. All three submarines had been incessantly hunted by the enemy, while the attempts of the submariners to torpedo their tormentors had been thwarted by the tactics of speed and evasive manoeuvring. A flat calm sea had also helped the enemy as the submarines' periscopes had been all too easily visible.

Lieutenant-Commander Herbert in the *D5* sighted a four-funnelled cruiser, the *Rostock*, screened by three destroyers on either bow and was able to approach unseen to within 600 yards of his target before firing both torpedoes. To his mortification he was not to be able to claim the first success against the enemy; both torpedoes missed.

Sunday 23 August
    D5 came in at 9.15 pm. . . . She must have seen the wake of the fish for she opened fire then and they dived to the bottom (120 feet they say!) and waited for two hours. At the end of that time they rose and found that one destroyer [the V157] was left to look for them, a thoughtful attention they did not require and they had to go deep again. When it was dark they surfaced and got under way on the engines and went off as hard as they could. Douglas [a Lieutenant-Commander who had retired before the war, been recalled and was then serving in the *D5* as the Third Officer] said they were so tired that they could not see properly and imagined

searchlights, flashes of guns and dark shapes every minute, so after they had gone about 12 miles they went to the bottom and remained there all night.

Lieutenant-Commander Max Horton in the *E9* had spent eight hours one day trying to get into position to torpedo one of the destroyers looking for him. At the end he had not even fired! The third boat was Leir's *E4* which easily beat the time for a long dive which had only recently been forced upon the *E7*. Leir's comment was brief: "After 24 hours dived breathing was nearly twice as quick, otherwise no difficulty at all."

At 3.0 am on Friday they tried to close in to the Bight and were soon surrounded by destroyers. It was flat calm and their periscope was soon seen and the destroyers never left them. At noon they just got their conning tower awash and Lockhart [First Lieutenant] opened the lid and put his head out. The first thing he saw was a torpedo boat rushing at him so he wasted no time and down they went! They were harassed all day but at 9.0 pm when it was dark they came up and this time Lockhart got his body out of the hatch when in the darkness he saw a black shape and then a flash and down he dropped and they dived again. They bottomed for the night at 110 feet. Next morning they rose very carefully to 20 feet and put the periscope up and there was a destroyer waiting for them, so they bottomed again and there they remained till 7 pm. All the time they were on the bottom they could hear the destroyer constantly passing over them and the propellers were so loud that it prevented them sleeping. So distinct was it that they could hear the rattle of the helm being put over. At first they thought it a chain sweep which was not a comforting thought.

Keyes' plan was to send a force into the Bight which would cut out the night patrols on their way home and the day patrols on their way out. If the enemy's larger ships came out to defend their patrols and drive off our raiding force they would be attacked by our submarines which would be lying in wait. In this Keyes was fully supported by Tyrwhitt. When proposing this plan to the Admiralty, he suggested that some cruisers of the Grand Fleet and the battlecruisers *Invincible* and *New Zealand* based on the Humber should be sailed to give support for the operation. However, Keyes was told that only the two ships from the Humber would be available, and so, in order to carry out the operation as soon as possible, it was decided to go ahead on this basis. Later, when Jellicoe was informed of what was to take place, he sailed Vice-Admiral Beatty's battlecruiser squadron and six 'Town' class cruisers to give their support. It was as well that he did, but by then both Tyrwhitt and his destroyers and Keyes in the *Lurcher* with the submarines were already at sea and no one in the Admiralty told them of the additional ships taking part in the operation. The result could have been tragic.

The initial plan also included provision for an attack by seaplanes of the RNAS on a cruiser thought to be lying in the western Ems estuary near Borkum, the aircraft being carried across the North Sea aboard the specially converted cross-channel ferry *Engadine*. The old cruiser *Sapphire* was to have gone along to escort the seaplane carrier, but in the event this part of the operation was cancelled. It is worthy of note, however, since it must surely rank as the original operation planned for an aircraft carrier.

Wednesday 26 August (Written at 8.45 pm.)

We leave at 0.30 am and ought to have a good show. The D2, D7 and D8 are going off the mouth of the Ems [the D7 did not go] and three seaplanes are being taken across there to attack a German cruiser known to be in the Huibert Gat, and our hopes are that she will run out and our D boats will scotch her. Three E boats are going out to take up positions on a line north and south of Heligoland by 4.0 am on Friday and three others to positions west of the island. I do hope and trust we shall at last have a smack (and a successful one) at them. Everybody has been so bored the last few days here with nothing to do and tonight everyone is on the grin except D1 and D4 who are staying behind, poor brutes. Well, I am ready; torpedoes fully charged today and the battery as well.

Eight submarines were sent into the Bight to be ready to take advantage of any moves that the German High Seas Fleet might make to counter this raid. They were positioned in two lines; three boats were on a line running north and south of Heligoland, with another three on a line about 40 miles to the west. Two more boats were positioned just to the north of the western and eastern Ems. The plan was that the inner line of boats would remain hidden while those on the outer line would make their presence known and draw the patrols out to where the destroyer flotillas coming up from seaward would be able to bring them to action. Should the German cruisers, or even heavier units, come out in support then they would have to run the gauntlet of the submarines on the inner line. The *Firedrake* left Harwich with the *E4, E5* and *E9* for the inner line at 10.30 pm on 26 August, followed two hours later by the *Lurcher* with the *E6, E7* and *E8* for the westward line, the *E7* going to a position almost due west of Heligoland itself.

Thursday 27th. (At sea)

Shoved off just after midnight and hung about in the harbour waiting for LURCHER. She came along after about 30 minutes and we formed into single line astern of her. We stopped this morning to close Smith's Knoll light vessel and waited for the D2 to join us from Yarmouth, and then off we went in divisions line abreast – first division E6, E7 and E8 – with LURCHER about two miles ahead of E6. Quite cold today on the bridge with no screen up. At 7.0 am LURCHER signalled our position and wished us good luck.

Commodore Tyrwhitt in the new light cruiser HMS *Arethusa*, in which he had hoisted his broad pendant for the first time less than 24 hours previously, sailed at 5 am on the 27th with thirty-one destroyers of the First and Third Flotillas. The first indication he had that any other forces were at sea was at 3.45 am the following day when four grey warships were discerned in the early light and were at first thought to be the enemy. However, the challenge was made, the correct reply received and the ships found to be the 'Town' class cruisers of the Grand Fleet. At this stage Tyrwhitt was told that, in addition, Beatty's battlecruisers were at sea. One disaster had thus been narrowly avoided, but still neither Keyes in the *Lurcher* nor the submarines knew of this additional support.

It was light at 4 am and the sun rose soon after. The sea was smooth, the sky overcast and the poor visibility was unaffected by the light north-westerly breeze. Just before 7 o'clock the enemy was sighted, the destroyer *G194*, and four destroyers, led by HMS *Laurel*, gave chase as the enemy turned towards Heligoland. For the rest of the morning and into the afternoon a confused and patchy battle was fought, the details of which form only the background to this story. The Germans lost three cruisers sunk, the *Ariadne, Köln* and *Mainz*, with two more damaged, a torpedo boat sunk and three damaged. For the British the battle did not fulfil the high hopes with which they started the day, nor did it prevent Keyes writing afterwards: 'It makes me sick and disgusted to think what a complete success it might have been.' While the British lost no ships, Tyrwhitt's new light cruiser, the *Arethusa*, and three destroyers, *Liberty, Laertes* and *Laurel*, were all badly mauled and were perhaps lucky that the arrival of the battlecruisers saved them from complete loss.

Interwoven with the actions of the surface forces were those of the submarines. Despite claims that the *Invincible* and *Queen Mary* had narrowly escaped torpedo attacks by German submarines, the U-boats were badly disposed and not in the area in which the British battlecruisers were operating. The U-boats were back in the inner Bight, far from the scene of the main actions of the day and presumably placed there in the belief that the British would sail in to attack the German coastal areas.

For the British submarines too it was a disappointing time, though generally far from dull. Although the *D2* and *D8* off the Ems saw the *Mainz* leave harbour with five torpedo boats at 10 am and made an unsuccessful attack, that was the last they saw of the German heavy units, their prime target. Unfortunately for the Germans, and for the British planners, the German battlecruisers were lying in the Jade River, not the Ems, and because of the state of the tide they were not able to cross the bar of the river before midday. In the course of their afternoon's foray they do not seem to have been sighted by the British submarines stationed around Heligoland because the *D2* and *D8* were in the wrong place.

From 7 am the *E4*, in her position south of Heligoland, could hear the sounds of battle to the west as the destroyer engagements came close. Eventually one of the German destroyers, the *V187*, came in sight and Leir dived, but was unable to make an attack and watched through his periscope as she was sunk by the British destroyers. Boats from HMS *Defender* were lowered to pick up the survivors, but while this was going on the cruiser *Stettin* arrived and the British destroyers were forced to leave. While Leir was shaping up to attack this tempting target, she too turned away. Twenty minutes later Leir surfaced and approached the *Defender*'s boats which were lying nearby. The submarine was able to take on board the British sailors who were unexpectedly saved from a prison camp. There was no room for the Germans on the submarine though Leir did take as "a sample" an officer, a petty officer and a stoker, leaving the others in the British boats and, ensuring that they had water, provisions and a compass, he gave them the course for Heligoland. In fact they were picked up only a few hours later by two of their own destroyers.

The *E4* later attacked the cruiser *Ariadne*, but without success, and soon afterwards saw the same cruiser again but this time she was too far away to attack and had the *Stettin* in company. After that the enemy were seen no more, though, from the sound of firing, the battle was often not far away. It had been an eventful and frustrating day for the *E4's* crew and their guests. The German officer admitted later that it was his first experience of going in a submarine and he had watched with great interest the attack made on the *Ariadne*.

The fears of both Tyrwhitt and Keyes were realized when first the *E6* and then the *E7* sighted the light cruisers of the Grand Fleet and believed them to be the enemy. But earlier that day Talbot had brushed with the enemy, sighting four destroyers in the three and a half hours after dawn. The first one found the *E6* on the surface with the German out of torpedo range. Eventually she signalled by light but the submarine declined to reply. When Talbot did dive the enemy promptly disappeared into the mist. When another destroyer was sighted Talbot tried to entice him towards the submarine by pretending to dive in poor trim, leaving his conning tower awash and the stern out of the water, but the enemy did not fall for this bait and he too disappeared into the mist. It was more serious when he worked to within 400 yards of four cruisers at about noon, making ready to fire his torpedoes. The events were recorded in his personal log:

> Sighted an action taking place between a German cruiser and some British destroyers, all approaching me out of the mist. Dived. I could not see these through the periscope but very shortly two lines of smoke appeared approaching me, and I heard a great deal of firing. I was between the two lines but nearer the northern line which I found to consist of three four-funnelled cruisers, which we all at once decided were German, as according to the programme we were to have no ships of that description in the area. I attacked; on their original course I could not have got in, but they altered course about five points [about 55°] to port together and I made what would have been a perfect attack on the last ship. At the last moments I had doubts as to their nationality, as shots were falling all round me from the cruiser I knew to be German, and I could find nothing else that these three ships could be firing at. I approached so close that I could actually see the red in the ensign, well within 400 yards, and knew them to be British, the SOUTHAMPTON class. We were closing so rapidly that I

could only get clear by diving under her, which I did. It was a very severe trial of my self-restraint, and I was thankful I had delayed firing till there was no possibility of doubt.

Later in the afternoon another cruiser came to the attention of the *E6*, and again Talbot's log tells the story:

. . . a large cruiser to the east approaching fast in a cloud of smoke. I turned round and attacked her, thinking she was chasing our destroyers. I passed down her port side at 300 yards' range, again waiting to see the colour of her ensigns, and again found her to be British and one of the SOUTH-AMPTON class, which are the most German-looking ships we have. It will be a wonderful thing if I get two more such opportunities for a certain hit.

For the *E7* the day was as busy and exciting as for any of the other boats.

Friday 28 August.
 The night passed quietly though my eyes are still aching from looking about so hard. I kept [watch] from 10.30 pm to 0.30 am and 2.30 to 4.30 am, and Feilmann kept the rest of the dark hours. I sent for Cunard at 3 o'clock to take star sights but he had no success on account of the very dark horizon. When I came on watch the sky had been very wonderful with the stars very bright. I thought that I had sighted a Zeppelin but it turned out to be a comet.
 At about 4.0 am, in that nasty half-light which is so tricky, I suddenly saw an object loom up and thought it was a sailing vessel. Then I got my glasses on her and she appeared to be a high-fo'c'sle cruiser coming straight for us. We dived without much waste of time and I opened up the stop valves of all the torpedoes and got them ready. While I was doing this Feilmann called me to the periscope: "What do you make of her?". There within range was one of the big German destroyers – V186 class. I rushed at the bow torpedo but as I was blowing water into the tube Cunard came forward and said "Too late". I nearly wept with disappointment. I had earlier decided to open all the stop valves at 4 o'clock as, in case of a leaky valve, I did not want to lose air from any of them during the night.
 I was very miserable for she was a sitting target going only at about 10 knots when Feilmann ordered me to get the bow tube ready again as the destroyer was returning. Sure enough she was, but we had to rush as she was now doing about 25 knots so Feilmann thinks. We were on her beam

about 150 yards off when Feilmann gave the order "Fire". I pulled the trigger of the firing pistol and heard the torpedo run out with such a cheery noise. I heard Feilmann shout "Take her down, 40 feet", and waited for the explosion. A lifetime seemed to pass and then I realized that it must have missed; it was laughable seeing everyone's expressions, all tense and with mouths open and then slowly they closed and a gloom settled on their faces. Feilmann said mine was quite comic.

From the German account it would appear that this was the *G194* which reported two torpedoes fired at her from the starboard beam, at a range of only 150 feet, where the periscope was sighted. No wonder they missed, for, however accurate Feilmann's shot at 150 yards (or 150 feet), the torpedo would not have taken up its assigned depth of six feet in such a short run. At that time it was believed that the Mark VI torpedo in use took about 250 yards to pick up its correct depth, and it was not until later that it was discovered that the distance was in fact much greater because the warhead was heavier than the peacetime practice head of the torpedo.

I went forward to console the torpedomen and they asked if I had heard the destroyer pass overhead. I had not, but a minute later there was a rushing rattling noise, apparently coming an inch or so over the hull. So close did it seem that I instinctively ducked my head, but on going to the depth gauge I found we were at 70 feet. It sounded like a mad dog chasing one, rattling over in such a furious hurry.

Half an hour later we came up, could see nothing of her through the periscope. After surfacing I climbed to the bridge and she was not in sight. We waited a bit and then took out the port tail clutch and charged the battery.

At 7 o'clock we heard firing to the northward and guessed it was our destroyers coming down and hoped that they had run across our friend. Soon the sounds were much nearer and we dived. Then we saw the FEARLESS and three divisions of destroyers [four in a division] coming down. We went to 40 feet and heard the westernmost division pass nearly overhead.

In fact, as has been related, the *Laurel* and her division opened fire on the *G194* shortly before 7 o'clock, the German turning towards Heligoland and taking the *G196* with her. The *Fearless* and the other destroyers also headed that way (passing over the *E7* as they did so) and ran into the enemy's 5th Flotilla which had been sent to hunt the

51

submarine reported by the *G194* – the *E7!* In the ensuing action several of the German ships were hit and only saved from greater damage by the arrival of the cruiser *Stettin*.

We surfaced at 7.35 am. Just after 10 o'clock we caught sight of four four-funnelled cruisers steaming south. The weather was very hazy and the sea not good for an attack, being too calm and with too few white horses. We dived and tried to approach this crowd but we were on their beam when we sighted them and a long way away so they were soon out of sight. At first I thought they might be German but later decided they must have been our 'Town' class.

Keyes himself in the *Lurcher* was at this time not far away. He had first sighted some light cruisers as early as 7.45 am, and not knowing them to be British he reported them to Tyrwhitt by radio as enemy, and then shadowed for an hour. Although he later began to wonder about the possible presence of British light cruisers he reported at 9.45 am that he was being chased by four enemy cruisers. Soon afterwards, in a temporary lift of the mist, he saw them more clearly and challenged them by searchlight, and was answered by the *Southampton*. Keyes was immediately concerned not only for the safety of the submarines, but also for that of that cruisers! Yet, despite his presence at the scene in the *Lurcher*, there was no way he could warn the submarines of this development.

(On the surface again.) All the firing was south of our position and we steamed towards it for 15 minutes, then stopped. The weather was still very hazy but the sun was making it quite warm and pleasant. The sea just rippled with scarcely ever a splash. We were keeping a mighty good lookout for ships coming out of the haze, and also for periscopes. At midday someone looked up and saw a seaplane coming over, she was not steering directly for us but we were not taking any risks and shot down to 70 feet, expecting a bomb at any moment. As a matter of fact I think it was one of ours – she had square wing tips and the Germans' have pointed ones.

Whatever the shape of the wing tips there were no British aircraft around! This was undoubtedly one of the seaplanes sent out, with the 5th Flotilla, after the *G194* had reported the *E7* earlier in the morning. Lying stopped on the surface in the midst of a battle seems very strange behaviour, indeed foolhardy. For, although it may save unnecessary use of the battery, it leaves the submarine a sitting target for attack by another submarine, and it will take much longer to dive in an emergency.

12.40 pm. Dived again for a big three-funnelled cruiser sighted on the port beam, but soon lost her from view in the periscope because of the poor visibility. Surfaced again. I had the intense satisfaction though of hearing big guns coming from her direction and knew she had met somebody. Soon saw splashes, enormous ones from 12 inch guns at least, so we guessed that INVINCIBLE or NEW ZEALAND were at work. Dived again and steered west in the hope of getting a shot at the German if she came near us. The nearest splashes must have been at least a mile off but directly the boat submerged we could hear the impact of the shells on the water as loudly as those from the cruiser which fired on us only a fortnight ago. Some of them made a curious rippling noise and I concluded they were bursting shell. The noise got no nearer and after ten minutes it ceased.

The cruiser sighted from the bridge by Hallifax was the *Köln*. She was sighted and chased by the British battlecruisers soon after 12.40. It took several salvoes to find the range but she was then hit by two 13.5-inch shells from the *Lion*, Beatty's flagship, which rapidly brought her to a standstill. At that stage another German cruiser came in sight, the *Ariadne*, and for a short while saved the battered *Köln* as the British ships shifted fire to the new target. The *Ariadne* was soon hit and left listing heavily and on fire. Beatty did not follow but turned his squadron back to dispose of the battered *Köln* and then to leave the area clear for Tyrwhitt's forces. The *Ariadne* sank about two hours later, the survivors being picked up by the *Danzig* and *Stralsund*. Recognizing the *Lion* at the head of the line of battlecruisers was the first intimation that Feilmann had that not only had the 'Town' class cruisers joined the operation but also some of Beatty's Grand Fleet battlecruisers.

At 2.05 pm sighted some 'Town' class cruisers and some destroyers going away from us to the north-west. We surfaced 15 minutes later, saw nothing and got under way on the engines steering for Smith's Knoll.

The battle was over, and like other British units the *E7* turned for home. She met up with the *E4* and the two submarines travelled together, swopping news as they went. In the evening they had some anxious moments when they met the *Invincible* and *New Zealand*, escorted by some destroyers, but the recognition procedures worked well. The *E4's* prisoners and the boats' crews from the *Defender* were taken off and the two battlecruisers proceeded on their stately way passing only about 100 yards from the two submarines. Next day in thick fog they came to Yarmouth and found the newspapers already full of details of the battle.

Keyes, as Commodore (Submarines), had had a hectic day dashing around the battlefield in the *Lurcher*. The ship's captain, Commander Tomkinson, an old friend of Keyes, even placed the *Lurcher* alongside the burning and sinking *Mainz* enabling many of her crew to be saved. It was no mean feat of seamanship by Tomkinson, but was this really the right place for the Commodore (S)? Once the battle had begun it was impossible to direct the submarines, and only placed him unnecessarily at risk, though this last factor would have weighed little with a man of Keyes' character. It was behaviour, though, that was to have repercussions, for when a similar operation was next under consideration Keyes was firmly told that for him to go off into the Bight was exposing himself to 'quite unjustifiable risks' and he was to stay ashore. Naturally Keyes protested, but to no avail. The Chief of Staff's order was confirmed by the First Sea Lord himself, and that was that, for the time being at least.

The result of this scrappy battle, greatly magnified at the time by the Press into a magnificent victory, lay not in the number of ships sunk but in its effects. In future the weight of British naval prestige dictated German naval thought, with the Kaiser, like Hitler after him, ever fearful to let the Navy engage in offensive operations in any but the most favourable circumstances. It was a view that soon began to infect the German Admirals, with the notable exceptions of von Tirpitz and Hipper. For the British the victory came at an opportune time for it provided something for the British people to cheer about at a stage when their army was in retreat in France and the enemy was in Brussels and was then approaching Paris and parts of the Belgian coast.

But there was little to cheer about for the submariners. Although the plan had only partially succeeded the submarines had neither had the chance to attack the main units of the German fleet which had not left harbour before the submarines had started for home, nor had they made any impact on the battle in those few attacks which they had carried out. In any case there was to be no peace and quiet after the battle for them. Seven boats were sent out on patrol in 1 September, while the *E7* was sent into the floating dock to try and stop a small but persistent leak into the after compartment from around the propellor shafts and to scrape and then paint the bottom which had become heavily overgrown with weed. Of the boats on patrol only the *E3* met with the enemy. They returned with two German airmen. The enemy seaplane had crash-landed with engine failure and the two airmen had spent many cold, wet and uncomfortable hours crouched on the upturned hull of their fragile machine when the submarine found and rescued them.

The officer, a sub-lieutenant I think, came up first. A nice looking fellow dressed like our flying chaps in gaiters and breeches, with an ordinary monkey jacket and a sort of oilskin cap. The seaman wore an airman's helmet and glasses [goggles] so what his real looks are I cannot say. They were marched through the work-shops onto the jetty where the soldiers took charge of them.

Later on the 4th the *E7*, with the *E4* and *E6*, were sailed from Harwich to Yarmouth, the latter port becoming a sort of jumping-off place for submarines going and coming from patrol. Consequently they expected to go out almost immediately, but were destined to stay in Yarmouth for some days. Another operation had indeed been planned and Leir, the senior commanding officer of the group, had the orders for the submarines. However, the day after their arrival he received instructions to burn the orders. At least their stay in harbour made for a change of both scenery and routine!

Saturday 5 September
   We have had a quiet day lying here. After lunch I went along the front with two other officers and we sat in deck chairs listening to the band, which was a nice way of spending the afternoon. One felt oneself back in civilization in comparison with the dull existence at Parkeston Quay.

Sunday.
   Some glorious weather. This afternoon Morris, Casey, (Third Officers of the E6 and E4) Cunard and I went along the sands where we sat for some time and then bathed. Its a fine beach for bathing from though the sand is rather trying when dressing.

Monday.

Glorious weather, very hot. I bathed this afternoon and listened to the band. Sitting there with the gardens crowded with women and children it was hard to remember that we were at war. However, a look at my companion's villainous beard and my own shabby uniform in a public place conveyed to us that times were unusual.

While waiting at Yarmouth the submariners heard of the loss of HMS *Pathfinder*, an old light cruiser and the flotilla leader of the Forth Destroyer Patrol. At first the loss was though to have been caused by a mine, the ship sinking in four minutes with the loss of most of her crew after a large explosion just off May Island in the Firth of Forth. In fact the cause was a torpedo fired by the *U21* (Korvettenkapitän O. Hersing) which struck the unfortunate *Pathfinder* in the forward magazine. The *U21* was one of two boats in the area; the other, *U20*, sighted nothing. One consequence of this bold incursion near Britain's new naval base at Rosyth was that six 'C' class submarines were sent to the Forth to reinforce the nine already there, with orders to search for, stalk, and, if possible, attack enemy submarines.

Since the battle on 28 August British submarines had returned to the Bight and reported that German patrol activity was undiminished. It also became known to the Admiralty that the German battlecruisers had been preparing to join the battle on that day but had been delayed. It was thought that a second raid into the area might achieve better results and one was therefore planned in which not only the Harwich forces would participate but also units of Jellicoe's Grand Fleet. On 3 September the Admiralty signalled him:

'Be prepared to meet not only battlecruisers but perhaps a division of the High Seas Fleet, or the whole Fleet. You should therefore be in a position with the Grand Fleet to take full advantage of so fortunate a chance.'

Originally intended for the 8th, the operation was postponed to the 10th. This was the delay that kept the three submarines in Yarmouth for longer than they expected.

Five submarines were to take part in this new venture, and by the time they were to sail early on the 9th all five were in Yarmouth. It was planned that the *E4, E6* and *E7* were to be off Heligoland – the first-named to the north and the other two to the south of the island.

The other boats, the *D2* and *D8*, were allocated positions off the Ems again.

> Destroyers are going to stir up the enemy as in the last operation but we are not going as decoys. We have to be in our positions by 2.30 am on Thursday at which time we bottom until 7 o'clock. Then we look out for the enemy's submarines. Our First Light Cruiser Squadron and the battlecruisers, six of them led by the LION, are supporting the Third Flotilla and it is hoped that the German fleet may come out to drive them off. Apparently they thought of coming out last time but were too late. That is what we count upon, and the whole of our Grand Fleet will be waiting within call to fall upon them. Great Scott!! If only it is successful!

Just as the *E7* was about to leave they found that the steering gear was jammed hard to starboard. Frantically Hallifax and the ERAs (Engine Room Artificers) sought to trace the trouble and repair it. Meanwhile the submarine was hauled ahead on the jetty so that the *E4* and *E6* could proceed. Leir instructed Feilmann to swop his orders with Jameson in the *D2*. Eventually the fault was found, the rudder freed and the *E7* dashed off, only some 15 or 20 minutes behind the *D2*, and determined to catch up and take her rightful place in the operation. In the early light of dawn they reached a rendezvous at a buoy at Smith's Knoll – the lightship had been removed the previous day – to find both the other *E* boats with the *Lurcher* and *Firedrake*, but no sign of the *D2*. The two destroyers, without, of course, the Commodore on the *Lurcher*, left the submarines in the afternoon after giving them their position and wishing them luck.

Not having seen the *D2* since she sailed to take the *E7's* position to the south of Heligoland, leaving the latter to go to the Ems if she could fix her steering, Feilmann's actions now seem unbelievable. Jameson was unaware that the *E7* had left Yarmouth so soon after him but Feilmann insisted on going to the position he was originally given and leaving a gap off the river Ems. It could have been an expensive mistake.

Thursday 10 September

Reached our position at 1.0 am and bottomed in 60 feet – we had expected more. Turned in and looked forward to a really good night instead of which I was woken every few minutes by the flies with which the boat is now swarming, settling on my face and even between my lips, nearly driving me mad. Cunard was cursing all night for the same reason.

Our orders were to stay on the bottom till 7 o'clock by which time the Third Flotilla and other ships would be clear to the westward. We came to periscope depth at that time having heard nothing all night and found a nice day with nothing in sight. Surfaced for a breath of air. Sighted two trawlers on the horizon.

Off the eastern Ems, soon after 7 o'clock on the morning of the 10th, Lieutenant-Commander T. S. Brodie in the *D8* sighted the light cruiser *Arcona*, a sister of the *Ariadne* so recently sunk in the battles on the 28th, together with a half flotilla of destroyers. As was so often the case, Brodie was not able to get into position to attack the German force, while they for their part forced the British submarine to go deep while being completely unaware of its presence. During the afternoon, with the *D8* this time on the surface, another submarine was sighted, also on the surface and at first Brodie thought this was the *E7*, out of position, but expected off the Ems, having swopped orders with the *D2*. In fact the other was the *U28* and Brodie soon realized his mistake and dived, as did the German. It was a hide-and-seek situation with the odds heavily against either boat being able to sight the other's periscope, and with neither boat having a hydrophone with which to be able to detect the other's noise. Then, quite by chance, both boats surfaced simultaneously, saw the other and dived again.

North of Heligoland the *E4* also engaged in an encounter with a U-boat when, soon after sunrise, Leir surfaced and found himself only 150 yards from the *U25*. Again it was a stalemate situation, and both boats remained dived waiting for the other to go away. Another opportunity for Leir came during the afternoon when he was able to stalk another submarine which he had sighted on the surface. Like so many other attacks this too failed as Leir had allowed himself to get too close before firing. It was a straight shot which must have passed under the *U23*, 'judging by the gesticulations on her bridge', as he reported later. Following on behind was a second submarine, the *U25* again, which opened fire at Leir's periscope while they both made off at high speed.

Two more U-boats and several destroyers were sent to the area to hunt the *E4*, as was the cruiser *Hamburg*. They failed to make contact, while the *Hamburg* herself was lucky to escape being torpedoed by the *U27* because of mistaken recognition, a fault not solely the prerogative of the British it would seem.

On a day with early morning haze that the still air did nothing to dispel and which grew quite warm as the sun rose higher, the sweep by the destroyers of the Third Flotilla started on time and proceeded as planned, except that it drew a blank. No contact was made with the enemy. The daytime destroyer patrols left Heligoland too late to be engaged by the early morning raid, while the night patrols were also missed. As the morning went by there was no German reaction to the British presence, and for all their high hopes when they had set out the British returned empty-handed. And, like the surface ships, the other submarines, including the *E7*, returned, having seen little other than a few trawlers.

> Surfaced again at 3.35 pm and when I went up I saw one of our boats to the north of us; it was the *E6*. She closed us and signalled "I suppose you have seen nothing?" We agreed and I asked them what they made of the trawlers and they thought, like us, that they were patrolling. *E6* said she was going to spend the night on the bottom and would leave for Harwich at 2 o'clock tomorrow afternoon.

> *Friday 11 September*
> Surfaced at midnight. Awful fuggy in the boat. Ventilated the batteries and 30 minutes later we bottomed again. The flies never worried us at all; we had slaughtered any amount during the day. Surfaced soon after dawn and found nothing in sight, but it was a bit misty and blowing fairly fresh from the south-west which raised a bit of a chop.

After the failure of the clutch to the flywheel regulator on the starboard engine, the latest in a long string of such incidents, the *E7* reached Yarmouth on the 12th after an unpleasant passage in bad weather. They went on to Harwich the following day. For the *E7* it was to be followed by a period in Chatham Dockyard where they were to try and repair the faulty clutch once and for all. It was a task that was to keep them from the war for most of the rest of September.

While the *E7* was in Chatham two events important in the history of submarine warfare took place. First, Max Horton in the *E9* sank the old light cruiser *Hela* when she was about five miles south of Heligoland steaming towards the Jade. Of the two torpedoes fired the first missed astern, while the second hit amidships. It was the first British submarine success of the war. The second occurred nine days later when Kapitänleutnant Otto Weddigen in the *U9* (a coincidence of numbers) sank three old British cruisers, the *Aboukir, Hogue* and

Cressy, in the space of eighty minutes. These were blows which showed emphatically that the submariners of both nations were actually a force to be considered, Weddigen's action in particular showing the world how the submarine could change the course of naval warfare. Such successes would vindicate the fruitless hours already spent on patrol, the hours that would be spent uncomfortably on the exposed bridges in the cold and storms of the coming winter, or the hours spent in the crowded and fetid atmosphere that is a submarine's after a few hours dived.

5

A Time Of Change

On 21 November, 1914, Lieutenant-Commander Archibald Douglas Cochrane RN assumed command of HMS *E7*, ending a series of events that must be without parallel in either World War among British submariners. But while the final scenes of this drama were taking place the *E7* herself saw little of operations or of Harwich, for most of the time she was in the Dockyard at Chatham having one defect or another repaired.

By early September the onward rush of the German armies in Flanders had taken them to the River Marne, within striking distance of the French capital, where General Galliéni stopped the retreat. By November the front line was taking a shape from the Swiss frontier to the sea near Dunkirk which was to change little for the next four years, leaving the British army holding a salient around the town of Ypres that will forever be associated with it. There were rumours that Russian troops were being sent to France to boost the strength of the Allied armies there, it being little appreciated how bare was the Russian arsenal. But the stories persisted, the troops had been seen, they must have been Russian: 'they had snow on their boots'!

Sunday 30 August
A territorial officer in charge of the guard told me that he believed that Cossacks had arrived in England and had been sent over to France from one of our East Coast ports. One of the destroyer officers told me the same thing. He said that a large number of Russians were being sent by sea from Archangel to Leith, thence by train to the east coast and on to France. Splendid show!

61

1 September

Seven boats were sent out today but where I don't know. I should think not to Heligoland again. My opinion is that they are covering the crossing of the Cossacks to France.

6 September

We heard that a Wilson liner had struck a mine in the North Sea and had sunk. The Harbour Master [at Yarmouth] says she was carrying emigrants but I suppose that the Russian troops are crossing from Hull, though of course that will not be given out. Poor fellows, there must have been a panic for I dont suppose half of them have ever seen the sea or know how to swim.

8 September

A press report from Rome stated that the Germans in France were retreating through Liège and that the Kaiser had moved his HQ to Metz. This was due to 250,000 Russian troops in France. I do hope its true and that the tide has really turned.

At this time spy mania was endemic throughout the country, as it was in all the Nations embroiled in the war. Numbers of innocent people watching, sketching, or even using cameras near troops or ships were hurriedly arrested and taken off to the nearest police station to explain their actions.

27 August

When we shoved off from Harwich [this had been just after midnight] Feilmann told me that a man had been seen letting off a carrier pigeon and that he had been caught by two soldiers, who, however, had to let him go. They reported it and an armed guard was sent to try and catch him. This was an unpleasant outlook for us as we are sure that the pigeon told of our departure.

5 September (at Yarmouth)

During the morning our signalman told Cunard (I was on the jetty) that two men on the opposite bank were sketching us. Cunard got a telescope to bear on them and one of them promptly tore some paper up and dropped it. We told the LIVELY and Baillie-Grohman manned a whaler to send across and land Cunard with some others while I crossed over in the ferry with Talbot and Jameson above them. Jameson and Talbot both took revolvers which protruded conspicuously from their pockets. When we got to them they acknowledged that they had taken photographs and they were taken to the LIVELY and then handed over to the Police.

9 September

Lockhart – on the E6 and just back from Zeebrugge – told me that they don't trifle with spies over there, anyone unable to account for himself or show a passport is chucked into gaol right away. He saw the Gendarmes hauling suspects off a train and marching them off without compunction. A pity we have not the sense to do likewise instead of having to get hold of correct police-court evidence to shut up a suspected spy.

Even senior officers were not above being involved in escapades of this nature. Both Keyes and Tyrwhitt were invited by Churchill to join him on a trip to Loch Ewe where he was to have discussions with Jellicoe and other Flag Officers from the Fleet in the flagship HMS *Iron Duke*. On their way by car between the railhead and this temporary fleet base they passed a large house with a high tower on which a searchlight had been placed. Churchill, ever one to be involved in an adventure, resolved to investigate on their way back after the conference. After all, it would be possible for a spy to signal details of the fleet's movements to a waiting Zeppelin from where they could be relayed to a U-boat. Arriving back at the house at 11.0 pm in pitch dark and pouring rain, Churchill, and a party of senior Naval Officers all by then armed with revolvers, demanded to see the owner. Churchill even demanded to see the searchlight and heard the, to him, unconvincing story that it was used to sweep the beats in the trees where it would glow on the eyes of the deer. Stalkers could then go to the most likely places in the morning. Various parts of the mechanism were taken away but it subsequently transpired that the unlikely story was quite true and that the light had been installed for this purpose some four years previously. The owner was indeed no spy, but a gentleman of unblemished reputation for patriotism. It should also be remembered that at this time no Zeppelins had been sighted anywhere in the country, let alone over the far west coast of Scotland.

An extension of the spy mania was the hysterical outburst, led by certain sections of the press, against anything German. Shops owned by people with German-sounding names had windows smashed and the contents looted. Even harmless dachshunds became the victims of the mobs' hatred. More seriously, it led to the resignation of Prince Louis of Battenburg, the First Sea Lord, on 28 October. It was a sad end to his career. He was replaced by Lord Fisher who was brought out of retirement to take over this post for a second time. Even Feilmann must have felt vulnerable because of his name, though it was

1916 before he dropped the final "n" and left it with a more English look.

Mines were fast becoming a hazard to the submarines patrolling in the Bight, both those of the Germans and also, later, those laid by the British. By International Law mines were meant to become inert once they broke free of their moorings in rough weather and started drifting. They certainly seemed to break their mooring wires often enough and the submariners could only hope that they became inert just as readily. A newly laid German minefield was discovered by Lieutenant-Commander Talbot in the *E6* in a dramatic way in late September when he fouled the mooring wire of a mine with his hydroplane while dived. On surfacing he found that the mine was securely held lying on the hydroplane, luckily with its horns pointed outboard. As the wire was still attached to it there was every probability that it was still live. One can well imagine the feelings of Talbot and his crew over the next 30 minutes while Lieutenant Freeman, the First Lieutenant, and Able Seaman Cremer carefully edged the mine free as the submarine pitched heavily in the swell. Their gallant efforts were later recognised with the award of the DSO and the CGM. The *D4* and *E7* had less exciting encounters with enemy mines in the same area.

> *Thursday 1 October,* off Norderney.
> At 10.30 am sighted land on the starboard beam. Very hazy with a nasty steep sea from all directions, the wind rising was from astern. Sometimes a sea would rise up to the level of the bridge and go with us for some moments, the whole boat submerged except for the bow and the top of the bridge. At 1.30 pm I sighted what I thought to be a black buoy a little on the starboard bow, but on closer inspection it proved to be a mine with five whiskers. We opened fire with rifles but with the heavy sea running it was only visible at intervals. Although hit several times we did not seem to be able to hit the whiskers to make it explode. Eventually, up went the mine, a black column of smoke and a jet of spray and water 150 yards high.

There were also false alarms.

> Just now screams of "Stop" – the engine room telegraphs were not working again – and then "Full astern port". I nipped up with a rifle and found that we had missed a large round mine, it could not be seen though and the lookouts swore it was a porpoise! Feilmann saw the animal shortly

64

afterwards and it proved to be a seal. Cunard said that he just saw something black bobbing in the water nearly ahead, and it gave him the shock of a lifetime.

Horton sank a destroyer on 6 October, his second success in two months. A destroyer is never an easy target and twice the *S116* had altered course just as Horton was about to fire, but finally he was left with an easy shot, firing two torpedoes at a range of 500 yards from the enemy's beam. When he next put the periscope up all that he could see was some 15 feet of the destroyer's bow sticking vertically from the water while her consort rushed to the scene to pick up survivors.

Only a week later Horton's *E9* was one of three boats which left Harwich in great secrecy to operate in the Baltic, passed through the enemy's patrols in the Kattegat and in the Sound between Denmark and Sweden to enter the Baltic and reach the Russian base at Libau. Lieutenant-Commander Nasmith in the *E11*, after desperate attempts to evade the enemy's patrols, had to turn back.

Next it was the turn of the Germans. On 16 October the *E3* (Lieutenant-Commander George Cholmley) sailed from Harwich to patrol off the western Ems. Two days later in mid-morning Kapitänleutnant Wegener in the *U27* sighted an object like a buoy which was soon identified as the conning tower of a submarine. It was the *E3* lying on the surface with about six of her crew on the tiny bridge looking out towards the shore, but none sighted the U-boat's periscope. Approaching to within 300 yards up-sun of the *E3* Wegener fired one torpedo. There was no mistake about running deep and the torpedo hit with fatal consequences.

Thursday 22 October
[On arrival] asked if there was any news and was told that the E3 had been sunk. She was due back last Tuesday but on Sunday the Germans reported that she had been sunk in a bay so we are afraid that it is true as her patrol position was off the western Ems. It is a sad business, Cholmley was such a nice fellow. If only we can find out that she was sunk by a submarine it will perhaps convince Feilmann that their submarines will attack us, and he will not be so ready to remain stationary on the surface with the bridge screens and other impedimenta up. When I spoke to him about it he answered in an airy way that their submarines do not intend to attack us with torpedoes. When I asked him why not he replied that they had not yet done so!

It has already been related that the *E7* spent most of the last half of the month of September in Chatham Dockyard having repairs to the starboard engine. By the end of October the boat was having to go back to Chatham, this time with cracks in the armatures of both main motors. In the meantime they had been back to the Heligoland Bight, taking their turn on patrol with other boats of the flotilla. By then there were few chances for any of them to meet with the enemy, and it was their lot to face the tedium of patrols in the worsening winter weather.

30 October
The E8 came in at noon with salt water in her battery and we expected to be sent out in her place, however I doubt if we will go after hearing Goodhart's report of the weather. There was a very heavy sea from the ENE, getting worse, so bad that he turned back deciding that his position off the Ems would be too dangerous. He already had traces of chlorine in the after end of one battery and when they had been steaming stern on to the sea for half an hour without a drop coming onto the bridge he thought it safe to lift the battery boards for an inspection. Scarcely were they up when a huge sea pooped them and water poured down the conning tower onto the exposed battery.

The weather endured in the Bight by the submarines gave rise to many songs and poems. One, written later in the war, but which is nevertheless just as true for the patrols of these early days, is reproduced here.

HANG ON

Two o' the morn, and a rising sea, I'd like to ease to slow,
But we're off on a stunt and pressed for time, so I reckon it's Eastward Ho!
So pick up your skirts and hustle along, old woman you've got to go —
Look-out, you fool. Hang on!

Up she comes on a big grey sea and winks at the misty moon,
Then down the hill like a falling lift, we're due for a beauty soon;
And here it comes – she'll be much too late – yes, damn it, she's out of tune —
Look-out, you fool. Hang on!

You can feel her shake, from stem to stern with the crash of her plunging bow,
 And quiver anew to the thrusting screw, and the booming engines' row;
 Then *rah-rah-rah* on a rising note – my oath, they're racing now —
 Look-out, you fool. Hang on!

The streaky water rushes by as the crest of the sea goes past,
 And you see her hull from the hydroplanes to the heel of her wireless mast
 Stand out and hang as she leaps the trough to dive at the next one –
Blast — !
 Look-out, you fool. Hang on.

In the hollow between she stops for breath, then starts her climb anew —
 "I can see your guns and wireless mast, old girl, but I can't see you,
 And you'd better be quick and lift again – she won't, she's diving through" —
 Look-out, you fool. Hang on!

The Lord be thanked, it's my relief – Cheer up, old sport, it's clean;
 No, just enough to wash your face – you could hardly call it green;
 A jolly good sea-boat this one is, at least, for a submarine —
 Look-out, you fool. Hang on!

At Parkeston Quay, where the submarines and destroyers were berthed with their depot ships, changes began to take place as though recognizing that the ships and their crews were to be there for a long time, and that the war would not be "over by Christmas". Two additional ships were acquired to provide accommodation; the *Vienna*, a Great Eastern Railways ferry, and the *Pandora* which had been completing for the Russian Navy. Sheds too had been built on the jetty to provide recreation for the crews; an early form of cinema was sometimes available as well as concerts given by visiting professional entertainers which provided a welcome change from the inevitable amateur theatricals and sing-songs. At nearby Dovercourt the Alexandra Hotel, or the nearer Cliff Hotel, became favourite spots for officers with a few hours of shore leave, providing concerts and a weekly Saturday afternoon tea-dance, or merely a place for a moments' peace and quiet.

Sport was organized and eventually all the traditional games were catered for. A nine-hole golf course proved very popular. Later still the traditional naval regattas also became part of the sporting scene. Finally, in case there was a chance that some were not taking any exercise, ships' companies were sent off, army style, on route marches. It all tended to be a greatly different experience from Scapa Flow, where for many months such facilities were non-existent.

There is little reference to the events leading up to Lieutenant-Commander Feilmann's departure from the E7 outside the diary of young Hallifax, his second-in-command, so that any perspective tends to be one-sided. It was obviously the end of a very unpleasant era for Hallifax, a period when the new stresses of modern war were added to the growing tensions between him and his Commanding Officer.

Despite his renown in fencing circles, his thespian successes and his apparent popularity among some fellow officers and their families, there seems to be little doubt that Feilmann was not an easy man to serve, a fact which Hallifax himself admits he was warned about by his colleagues when first appointed to the E7 in 1913. There is also little doubt that, whatever the relationship between the Commanding Officer and his First Lieutenant in the months before the war, they both managed to work together and contain any dislike within the usual bounds of service discipline. Many readers who have served in one or other of the services will have experienced a similar relationship some time during their career, and will have coped with the situation knowing that time will almost certainly bring changes sooner or later. With the outbreak of war time could no longer be counted as an ally, while there were the added tensions caused not only by war but also by the fact that, as submariners, they were taking part in a war for the first time.

Hallifax became aware of Feilmann's limitations quite early on and became increasingly concerned over their possible effect on him in particular and the E7 in general. For his part it would seem that

Feilmann became more and more irritated by the attitude adopted by his junior who must have let his feelings show all too clearly. Hallifax makes several references in his diary to Feilmann's lack of professionalism, not only in his ignorance of the layout and working of the submarine but also in matters such as leaving secret papers lying around in his cabin in the *Maidstone*. Reference has already been made to the meeting between the *E5* and *E7* and the German cruiser *Strassburg*. Feilmann's indifference at the time was matched later in harbour when replying to the question by another commanding officer why he hadn't dived sooner, 'Oh, I couldn't do that, Benning was the senior officer!'

Amid a host of little incidents, which in these circumstances tend to assume an importance beyond their true worth, there was the inference that on occasions Feilmann had had too much to drink, even at sea. There were two other habits which put the submarine at risk. Although the *E7* had a Third Officer, Cunard, he was inexperienced and was allowed to keep few watches on his own. As a consequence Feilmann, as Commanding Officer, was obliged to keep watches, sharing the load with his First Lieutenant, an onerous task for both officers, but the more so for Feilmann when added to all his other responsibilities in enemy waters in wartime. Around the primitive bridge a canvas screen could be lashed to give some protection from the elements to those on watch, but this screen had to be taken down before the boat dived. Feilmann liked his comfort – if even such meagre protection could be called comfort in the stormy waters of the Heligoland Bight in autumn – and often had the screen rigged while he was on watch. Sitting behind it on a camp stool gave some respite from the weather, though it did little to improve either alertness or the chances of sighting the enemy before being sighted by him.

This was compounded by his habit of lying stopped while on the surface even though in enemy waters. Apart from making life slightly drier and warmer for those on the bridge there was nothing to recommend this dangerous practice. He was convinced that he would sight another surfaced submarine at least at the same time as the *E7* was sighted, while a dived submarine was unlikely to be able to carry out a successful attack on him. This surprising attitude continued even after Leir's attemps to sink the two U-boats in the Bight in early September, even after the loss of the *E3* and even after another unsuccessful attack on the *B3* off Dover.

69

While all this was of growing concern to Hallifax, what could he do? It must be remembered that discipline in 1914 was much stricter and less enlightened than today, and to even consider reporting one's captain for malpractice was a very serious step indeed.

17 October
Every time we go out I hate it more and more and get very nervy. If only F would give me a real damning bit of evidence of criminal stupidity or get really drunk instead of merely sozzled I would go to the Commodore. As it is I have to go and stick it as best as I can.

Eventually, after some quiet talks with Cunard and another of the First Lieutenants of the flotilla, Hallifax decided that he would have to seek advice and chose to approach Talbot of the *E6*. One can only guess at his true feelings at taking such a momentous step, but it can not have been an easy decision to take.

After that I went to my cabin and thought hard about seeing Talbot. At last I got as far as walking up and down outside his door, then tossed a coin and let it decide for me. I told him I wished to speak to him and ask his advice about another Skipper and that if he would rather not hear it to say so. He told me to go on. I told him absolutely everything. He was not, I fancy, astonished about F's lack of knowledge but was so in regard to his drinking at sea. He was awfully nice about it and we talked it over for some time. He said "Of course a fellow like that ought to be hauled out of the job at once."

Later the same day Talbot asked Hallifax to play golf with him during which the matter was discussed again without any conclusion being reached. It is interesting to note that while Talbot records the golf match with Hallifax in his own diary he makes no reference to the more important matter.

Nothing then happened except that the *E7* spent a few more days in the Bight on patrol. It must have been an anxious time for Hallifax as he thought about the situation and the possible disciplinary troubles for himself. Had he done the right thing in telling all to Talbot? In fact he decided that on his return to Harwich he would have to speak to Leir, who was the senior Commanding Officer, in much the same vein that he had with Talbot. This he did on 30 October, and this time the response was rapid. Within hours he was taken in to see Captain Waistell, the Captain of HMS *Maidstone* and Keyes' deputy.

I am hanged if I can define my feelings, partly elation at having taken the step, and a certain amount of . . . remorse? No, not remorse, but its a nasty thing to have to do. This afternoon I plucked up enough courage to speak to Leir about Feilmann. Having done so I am doubly glad that I first went to Talbot for Leir is a difficult person to speak to, as I thought he would be. However, he was very nice about it and said I was perfectly right to speak to him and he would see into the matter.

After tea Leir came into the smoking room and beckoned to me and led me up to Captain Waistell who said "I hear that you have a very distasteful matter to report. I know how unpleasant it must be for you but I am very glad you have brought it up and consider you to be quite right to do so." I then repeated all the facts to him.

The following day he was taken in to see Keyes himself and once again had to go through the whole sorry catalogue. Yet again Hallifax was assured that he was correct in bringing the matter to the attention of senior officers. And there Hallifax had to leave it as the submarine returned to Chatham for repairs and he was left to serve an awkward time with Feilmann who must have sensed something was going on, though strangely he was not aware of the serious allegations against him for some time. Neither what Keyes thought, nor the action he took, is mentioned in any of his papers. However, in mid-November Feilmann was summoned to the Admiralty and re-appointed to the command of the old submarine *C32*. This was very much a public disgrace for Feilmann, as command of the C class submarines was for the more junior and first-time Commanding Officers, and not for one as senior as him, recently in command of an operational "Overseas" boat. By a twist of fate he had only recently been Mentioned in Despatches for his part in command of the *E7* during the Battle of Heligoland Bight.

Feilmann thus leaves this story. It is unfortunate that Keyes' views are not available, for it is perhaps significant that he was not removed completely from the submarine service. Indeed, after only a short period in the *C32* Feilmann was appointed in August, 1915, to the *E31* which was then building at Greenock. From this submarine he was promoted Commander and sent in command of the new steam-driven submarine *K14*. But again his career becomes an enigma. In February, 1917, when writing a report on Feilman (as he was then known) the same Captain Waistell commended him for his work as Senior Submarine Officer of the flotilla, and noted that he had a thorough knowledge of his boat, but with a warning note concerning the size of his wine bill. His First Lieutenant in the *E31*, Douglas Gavin, volunteered to go with Feilman to stand by the *K14*, then building. *E31's* Torpedo Gunner's Mate, Arthur Hime, was another who followed his Skipper to the *K14*, as did several other volunteers. Yet Ronald Blacklock, who took over command of the *E31*, noted that the boat was generally in poor condition, the crew slack and inefficient.

Feilman again fell foul of authority in 1917 and was removed from both the *K14* and the submarine service. He finished the war organizing convoys, being commended for his work and was again Mentioned in Despatches. He retired in 1920.

The *E7* had a new Commanding Officer. Archibald Douglas Cochrane was born in Springfield, near Cupar, in the County of Fife on 8 January, 1885. He sprang from an ancient and famous Scottish family, his forebears for some six hundred years having served with great distinction, and often in high rank, in both the Army and the Navy. His father was the first Baron Cochrane of Cults and he was a cousin of the 13th Earl of Dundonald.

Destined for the Royal Navy himself, it seems natural that Archibald Cochrane should have developed a tremendous respect and admiration for his great-grandfather, the 10th Earl of Dundonald, perhaps the most famous member of this famous family. Thomas, Lord Cochrane, as he is better known, was born in 1775 and his life story ranks with that of Nelson and is more extraordinary than those of the fictional heroes Hornblower, Ramage or Bolitho. With a small coasting brig of 158 tons, HMS *Speedy*, which he described as 'little more than a burlesque of a vessel of war', he harried French and Spanish shipping in the Mediterranean, seizing over 50 vessels, including a frigate many times his own ship's size, and halted the French advance into Catalonia for two weeks. Later, when in command of HMS *Imperieuse*, he brilliantly destroyed a French Squadron in Basque Roads after an attack by fire-ships. Lord Cochrane then entered Parliament as a radical reformer determined to try and stamp out wholesale corruption within the Admiralty, the Royal Dockyards and elsewhere. Such a man made many enemies who used the system to secure his disgrace within the navy and later his conviction for fraud on the Stock Exchange. Going abroad, Lord Cochrane continued his career commanding in turn the Chilean, Peruvian, Brazilian and Greek navies in their Wars of Independence.

The accession of King William IV allowed him to return to England, establish his innocence of any fraud and resume his career in the Royal Navy becoming an Admiral of the Fleet and the Commander-in-Chief of the America and West Indies Squadron. He died in 1860. It was a career with which that of his later kinsman was to show many similarities.

Archibald Cochrane entered the Royal Navy at an early age, joining the *Britannia* at Dartmouth in September, 1899. While at Dartmouth he was a contemporary of Charles Benning, already met with in this story as the Commanding Officer of the *E5*, of Gilbert Kellet, a friend of Feilmann and in 1914 commanding the new submarine HMS *S1*, and of John Codrington, Hubert Vaughan-Jones and Brownlow Layard who were all to become submariners.

Leaving the *Britannia* with time gained as a result of his examinations, his report stated that he should get on in the service if he worked hard enough. Good examination results as a Midshipman and Sub-Lieutenant saw him promoted to Lieutenant on 30 July, 1906, by which time he had volunteered, and had been accepted, for service in submarines.

In those days there was little in the way of formal instruction for young officers arriving to join the submarine service. Very quickly they were sent to a boat to learn at sea from their Captain, the quality of their instruction depending greatly on the knowledge of the Captain and the keenness and ability of the pupil. Cochrane set about learning how the submarine and its various components worked.

It became the custom for submarine officers to spend at least two years in surface ships to gain experience of general service conditions after an initial spell in submarines. Generally it was welcomed by the submariners as they had no wish to be regarded as a navy within a navy and perhaps become ineligible for higher command within the fleet. It was no surprise, therefore, to Cochrane when in 1910 he was appointed to the cruiser *HMS Defence* and exchanged the white submarine sweater for the more dignified frock coat, cocked hat and sword. By coincidence he was with the younger Hallifax during the tour of India by the King and Queen.

He returned to submarines in 1912 when he was appointed in command of the *D1*, the same boat in which he spent the opening months of the war. Despite the boat's reputation for unreliability, with her experimental diesel engines, he patiently kept her seaworthy first operating from Dover and then Harwich. During October he carried out a patrol off the Ems from which he brought back much useful information on the enemy's patrols. Working close inshore and with great daring, he found the channels constantly occupied by destroyers and trawlers, though, perhaps because of Horton's success against the *S116*, they did not seem particularly aggressive. For this patrol in particular he won Keyes's approbation and was subsequently Mentioned in Despatches.

At the end of October he was moved first from the *D1* to the *D7*, and then, just three weeks later, to take command of the *E7*, Brownlow Layard taking over from him, leaving the *C32* to do so.

> I was rather frightened of Cochrane. In the DEFENCE I never quite knew how to take him as he is very reserved at times. I know he is a mighty good Skipper.

6

It Wasn't Over By Christmas

WITH COCHRANE IN command the *E7* returned almost immediately to
Harwich. Cochrane set about imposing his own character on the boat
and crew, while Hallifax had a Commanding Officer he could respect
and now had to show that he himself was worthy. It would be a testing
time for all. There was, however, one other change – Sub-Lieutenant
Ian Twyman came to the *E7* in place of Cunard, having been with
Cochrane in the *D1*.

23 November
   Twyman is our new Third Officer. He was in the D1 and Cochrane
arranged for him to come to us. He says that Cochrane is a weird fellow to
serve with as he seldom says much, but that he would not leave him for
anything. He added that he was as cool as a cucumber and the tighter the
fix he gets into the cooler he gets. I am glad to start a new volume of the
diary with my first day at sea with Cochrane and feel like burning the rest
and forgetting that part of the war. The future will be very different.

1 December
   Rumours of a "stunt" coming off in the next few days. I hope that it is
so. I do feel different now with regard to going out; before, I used to dread
it more each time, but with Cochrane I would go anywhere. [Later]. The
"stunt hizz" was a hizz!

7 December
   With a Skipper like Cochrane I am beginning to find out how ignorant
in certain matters I am because he points out things about which I have
never troubled. Had I gone on with F I should have continued to think I
knew a lot, which I did compared to him, and should have gone on in the

75

old way till I got a command. Now I shall pick things up which will be invaluable to me later. (And how!)

By the end of November intelligence suggested that most of the High Seas Fleet was assembled in the harbours of the German North Sea coast and that an offensive operation was likely. It seemed to the Admiralty that there was a chance of bringing the enemy to action if their movements could be forestalled by the Grand Fleet, Tyrwhitt's force from Harwich and perhaps a seaplane attack on the Zeppelin sheds at Cuxhaven. Neither the Commander-in-Chief nor Tyrwhitt was in favour of trying to take the seaplane carriers into the Bight in November when the weather was almost certain to be unsuitable. Nevertheless the *Engadine* and *Riviera*, each with three seaplanes embarked, were included in the plan. At first no submarines were included in the operation order but were later added in order to patrol close to Heligoland to intercept the enemy if he came out in pursuit of the British force. They would also be available to pick up any pilots who had to come down in the sea, a new role for the submarines and one which was to become far more common during the Second World War. For this operation the *D2, E5* and *E15* were designated to take part.

The submarines sailed on the morning of 22 November to be in position on the 24th. The weather was at its winter worst with a strong easterly gale. Anchoring for the night rather than trying to navigate the unlit Haisborough swept channel in the dark in such conditions, the three boats had a most uncomfortable time. Seas were breaking over their conning towers and the *E5* pitched so badly that the hydroplanes were strained and the guards torn from the hull, causing a bad leak. At daylight they tried to proceed, but at such slow speed they soon realized that they would not be able to play any part in the operation. So they returned to harbour. Besides the damage to the *E5*, the heavy seas caused the loss of Lieutenant-Commander Jameson, the Commanding Officer of the *D2*, who was swept from the bridge while on watch and drowned. It is ironic that only a few days earlier he had been offered the command of the *E7* to replace Feilmann, but had asked to stay in the *D2* until the new *E16* was ready.

Despite the weather experienced by the submariners both the Grand Fleet and Tyrwhitt's force sailed with the seaplane carriers to keep their rendezvous for the operation. Surprisingly there was an improvement in the weather and as the winds began to drop hopes rose that it would be possible to carry out the operation. But it was only a lull and at last the Admiralty cancelled the operation and ordered the forces back to harbour.

Two days later, with renewed indications of enemy activity around Heligoland, the *E15* and *D2* were sent out again to investigate. Replacing Jameson in the *D2* was Lieutenant-Commander C. Head, who in more peaceful days was also an enthusiastic amateur aviator. The *E15* reached Heligoland in weather that showed the correctness of the decision to cancel the seaplane raid. A severe south-westerly gale now hindered the patrols. Lieutenant-Commander Brodie in the *E15* (he had earlier commanded the *D8*) shaped up to attack two small steamers but forbore to fire at the last moment when he sighted their merchant ensigns and realized that he would be unable to surface, order them to stop and then see their crews safely into boats before trying to sink the ships. In a worsening gale he started back for Harwich, at one time making only two knots into the teeth of the gale, and also losing a man overboard.

2 December

E15 came in this afternoon, she had been over to Heligoland. They met with appalling weather on the return journey which commenced on Saturday and took three days. One day their average speed was about one knot. Their bridge stanchions were knocked down and Brodie has two black eyes and his RNR Sub-Lieutenant has one.

Of the *D2* nothing more was seen or heard. German sources reveal no clue as to her fate and it must be assumed that she became a victim of one of the many drifting mines set loose by the storm. It was a sad loss for the Harwich flotilla.

Among the many newcomers at Harwich at this time was *HMS S1*, the first of Keyes' foreign-designed but British-built submarines to be completed. She was commanded by Lieutenant-Commander G. Kellet, a friend of Feilmann's and, having been completed on the first day of the war, had spent the intervening time working with the submarines on the Dover patrol. Also, the French arrived. For some time the French had been keen for their submarines to take an active part in the war in the North Sea, and had offered the newly completed *Gustave Zédé* as an additional unit to Keyes' flotilla. However, once it was appreciated under what conditions the submarines were required to operate in the Heligoland Bight it was decided that she was not sufficiently worked up. Eventually, on 3 December the steam-driven *Archimede* arrived at Harwich escorted by the destroyer *Sagaie*. Other French boats were already working with the Dover patrol and it was expected that more would soon follow the *Archimede* to Harwich.

3 December
   This forenoon the French boat arrived – a curious looking boat with tubes on deck. I wonder how they will manage about sitting on the bottom at night, or even at 90 feet. Their torpedo tails will collapse I should think. She carries three officers. Her surface displacement is 600 tons and she has steam engines with a stubby funnel just abaft the bridge. Just forward of the funnel is a galley. I should think she will be very wet in a seaway.

Hallifax's concern for the French submarines torpedoes was occasioned by the fact that she had four fitted externally without tubes and only one internal torpedo tube. Her surface displacement was actually 570 tons, making her smaller than the British E class. With much of her internal space taken up with the steam boilers and engines, the externally fitted torpedoes were a means of saving space. The "drop collar" release gear in which they were held was the brain child of the Russian engineer Drzewiecki, but in practice it proved too delicate and tempermental and its use had been all but abandoned by the end of the war. In any case these torpedoes could not be fired unless the submarine was dived. The only British submarines to use this device were some of the E class which were sent to operate from Russian bases in the Baltic, where in 1915 a shortage of British torpedoes forced them to try out this system with Russian weapons.

   The German submarines had been remarkably unsuccessful in detecting the Grand Fleet during any of its sorties from Scapa Flow. Even the movements of the Fleet after the German raid on Yarmouth – which had led to the accidental loss of the *D5* on one of our own mines just off Yarmouth – was unknown to the German staff. Consequently Admiral Hipper proposed that his battlecruisers should carry out a raid against British shipping known to be still using the southern Scandanavian ports. This, he thought, might provoke another sortie by the Grand Fleet. However, he was overruled and another Yarmouth-type bombardment and minelaying raid was ordered with Hartlepool and Scarborough as the targets. It is difficult to understand just why these towns were chosen to be the targets for four battlecruisers, an armoured cruiser and five light cruisers, the former being of only minor military importance and the latter none at all. More worthwhile targets for such a force can easily be imagined.

Thanks to a Russian coup in recovering the secret German basic code book from the wreck of the cruiser *Magdeburg*, one copy of which was sent to London, the British had begun breaking the German signals. On the night of 14/15 December the Admiralty became aware that the Germans were preparing some move against the east coast, though just where they would strike was not clear. Nevertheless, the Admiralty ordered the Grand Fleet to sea to counter the threat, while Commodore Tyrwhitt's forces were to concentrate off Yarmouth ready to move towards the enemy when his movements became known.

At Harwich there were fourteen submarines available for operations. Eight, including the *E7*, were to be spread along a line running SSE from a position 30 miles NW of Terschelling, the *Archimede* being the inshore boat on the 10-fathom line off the Dutch coast. With them went the faithful *Lurcher* and *Firedrake*, the former with Keyes himself embarked. Prince Louis, when First Sea Lord, had stopped Keyes from going to sea but Fisher now held that post and Keyes no longer felt constrained by the order and was taking the first opportunity of going to sea again. Remembering the poor performance of the submarines' radio receivers and in particular their short range, it seems a strange place to have deployed the submarines where they could play little part in closing the door to the returning German forces in all but one of the options open to them, and from intelligence it was a most unlikely one. Indeed, once they were clear of Harwich there was little chance of Keyes, even when on the spot himself, being able to order any redeployment to better patrol areas.

15 December

We shoved off at 3.10 pm, all the E boats except the E6 which was damaged, and the ARCHIMEDE. We went in pairs, the E7 with the E2, by the North Hinder route. A filthy night, raining hard and as dark as sin. The gyro compass was not exactly a success as the repeaters will not keep step and we found ourselves a long way off course.

16 December

We stopped and dived for a trim. As the weather was much better we could have a smoke on deck. Apparently we have come over on account of a report that a German battle fleet is expected to make a dash at our ships bombarding the Belgian coast.

Shortly after 8 am on 16 December the Germans began bombarding Hartlepool from the two battlecruisers *Seydlitz* and *Moltke*, the targets including the coastal batteries, docks and gas works, though considerable damage was done to the town and there were over 500 casualties, most of them civilian. Some damage was done to the German ships by the return fire of the batteries. In harbour was the submarine *C9*, specifically based there to help defend the area in just this sort of eventuality, together with two old light cruisers, *HMS Patrol*, with the Senior Officer embarked, and *HMS Forward*. All coastal patrols had been warned to be specially alert that morning and, weather permitting, all vessels were to be at sea before daylight. However, the weather was bad with a heavy sea running, making the bar dangerous in the low state of the tide, and only four small destroyers of the *Patrol's* flotilla had gone to sea. As soon as the sound of firing was heard the *Patrol, Forward* and *C9* began to get to sea. As the *Patrol* started to work her way out of harbour shells were already falling on the docks and she came under heavy fire in the entrance. As she got clear she was struck by two shells from the heavy cruiser *Blücher* and then grounded on the bar, only being saved from far worse damage as the German ships broke off the action when they came under fire from the shore battery. The *Patrol* was followed by Lieutenant C. L. Dering in the *C9* who was also straddled in the harbour entrance and forced to dive. The water was too shallow and she grounded but managed to bump her way over the bar, helped by the heavy swell; but she was unable to close the enemy to make an attack. The *Forward* left harbour unscathed but was not able to keep in contact with the German ships as they disappeared into the mist.

At Scarborough the German ships met with no opposition, caused over 100 casualties and again did considerable damage to the town, without the excuse of either harbour or coastal batteries to give justification to the action. As the Germans retired they fired another fifty rounds into the small town of Whitby. At this stage it would appear that the closing British squadrons were bound to catch and overwhelm the German raiders. It is no part of this story to follow in detail the various moves of each side that day; suffice it to say that, despite the overall superiority of the British ships, despite the advantage given to the Admiralty by intelligence and by the codebreakers, another magnificent opportunity for victory was lost. Criss-crossing the German tracks, the British were so often so near without actually sighting the enemy, and when he was sighted he was either lost in the mist or by some inept command decisions and ambiguous signalling.

By the time the Germans were beginning their bombardment of the English town Keyes' submarines had taken up their positions off Terschelling. Now the full extent of the inadequacy of the submarines' radio equipment was realized, for at about 10.30 am the *Lurcher* intercepted a faint signal that the Germans were off Scarborough. If this was so then the submarines were poorly placed to intercept the enemy on his way home. Even Keyes in the *Lurcher* was out of touch with the Admiralty and had to send the *Firedrake* back towards Yarmouth for new orders while he used the *Lurcher* to try and collect his submerged submarines ready to act as soon as the *Firedrake* returned.

By 5 o'clock he had collected only the *E10, E11, E15* and the *Archimede* who were then sent to form a new patrol line to the west of Heligoland. There it was hoped they would be able to intercept Admiral Hipper's ships or the supporting High Seas Fleet as they headed back to their bases. In the dark and in steadily worsening weather the *Lurcher* sailed up and down the original patrol line off Terschelling as Keyes hoped to be able to contact more of his submarines, while the *Firedrake* stood to the west to pass signals to the Admiralty informing them of the new positions of the submarines. But it was a forlorn hope, for the orders given to the submarines before sailing from Harwich had instructed them to stay only until nightfall when they were to return to Harwich, and eventually Keyes accepted that this was what had happened and he too stood to the south-west for home.

Of the four submarines off Heligoland only the *E11* (Lieutenant-Commander M. E. Nasmith) actually sighted the enemy. After picking up the dark shape of the island in the early hours of the 17th, Nasmith altered course towards the Weser light vessel and saw nothing of Admiral Hipper's battlecruisers which returned to their anchorage in the Jade River before dawn. However, at 7.20 he sighted four German destroyers which were covering the passage of some of the German battle fleet from the Elbe to the Jade. Some twenty minutes later the German 1st Battle Squadron hove in sight – two ships followed after an interval by two more. Fifty minutes later he fired his starboard beam tube at the *Posen* at a range of 400 yards. Surely he must hit, surely after all the earlier failures the torpedo must run at the correct depth? But no. This time the weather was to foil the attack. In the heavy swell the submarine was rolling even at periscope depth and this caused the torpedo to run wild, probably to go too deep, and to miss again. Another battleship passed over him causing him to take the *E11* deep to avoid being rammed, and when returning to periscope depth to try and attack one of the ships of the second pair he lost trim in the swell and broke surface, a sight the Germans could not help seeing. They all left the area at full speed with the *E11* unable to do anything more to attack them.

Sunday 20 December.

At noon E11 came in and the news makes one want to weep. They had sighted columns of smoke and soon after some German destroyers appeared followed by the German fleet in single line ahead, about one mile apart and steaming very fast and zig-zagging. By that time there was a heavy swell and they were rolling 6° to 7° each way. They got ready to fire at the first ship but she altered towards them. As they were about to fire the bow tubes at the second ship she too zig-zagged and they had to fire the beam tubes. At the moment of firing they were rolled 7° one way so that the torpedo would either have gone very deep or broken surface and then dived to the bottom. It was impossible owing to the enemy's speed to wait for the boat to be on an even keel. When the next ship thundered over them she made such a deafening noise they could not hear any orders at all.

However, it was left to the *Archimede* to have the most eventful patrol, although it was the elements rather than the Germans that she had to fight. She arrived off Heligoland with her oil-fired boilers throwing the usual dense column of smoke into the sky mixed with a display of sparks that augured no good for submarine operations. In a rising gale and with the barometer still falling, a heavy sea twisted the forward hydroplanes so that they could not be used, while a second sea knocked the retractable funnel out of its guides. This was a serious defect for if the funnel could not be lowered then the great watertight hatch could not be shut and the submarine could not dive, and even on the surface it meant a continual surge of water down the funnel and into the boat. The *Archimede* was no longer a submarine and was virtually unarmed in hostile waters for her external torpedoes could not be fired unless the boat was dived. Luckily the storm became a friend for it kept the German patrols in harbour as the crippled submarine crept back towards her English base into the teeth of the gale.

On the *Archimede* at this time was Godfrey Herbert, temporarily without a boat of his own following the loss of the ill-fated *D5*, there to give advice and help to the French on their first operational patrol in enemy waters. Now Herbert found himself in a line helping to pass buckets from hand to hand, baling out the water wich surged into the boat with every passing wave. The story is told that one of the French crew said to him, '*Il fait très mauvais temps, Monsieur.*' Herbert's reply – in French accented as only an Englishman can – '*Oui, mais après le mauvais temps vienne le beau temps*' became an instant catch-phrase among the crew, being shouted in chorus by the bucket line whenever there was a particularly heavy inrush of water.

Despite fears that they would have to make for Holland and there be interned for the duration of the war they eventually reached the English coast off Cromer and went on to Yarmouth and then Harwich. Alongside the *Maidstone* they made temporary repairs which at least made the boat seaworthy again before she returned to France for a refit. It remained the only operational patrol by a French submarine in the Heligoland Bight throughout the war.

The *E7's* role had been uneventful and she had returned to Harwich leaving her billet off Terschelling on the evening of the 16th in accordance with her orders without having seen the *Lurcher* or any of Keyes' attempts to attract attention.

16 December

Sighted nothing the whole afternoon and at 4 o'clock the E2 closed us and we got under way and followed her. We lost her in the dark two hours later – I was glad as it is very tiring having to follow a boat on an inky black night when they only flash a light at you once every five or ten minutes. It began blowing hard from the westward and raining heavily during the evening. Very cold.

17 December

Called at midnight and kept watch till 4 o'clock – four hours is too long in a boat where one can't walk about. In the winter you get chilled to the marrow and the cold wind nearly blinds you. By the end of the watch my eyes felt like red hot coals. It was pitch dark but had stopped raining thank goodness. Later we eased to slow ahead as we had not picked up the North Hinder light and Cochrane said we would go slow till daylight. When that came there was nothing in sight so we went on at 12 knots but stopped when we saw breakers ahead, and then sounded. 15 fathoms. We went on round the shallow patch and after a time took another sounding – 17 fathoms. Still nothing in sight so we went again at 10 knots. Soon afterwards we sighted the Shipwash. We had come across the latest minefield! Safest route I think as the mines probably drift from their proper positions and into the so-called safe channels!

It was the little *C9* at Hartlepool who had come nearest to the enemy and Keyes found it most galling that she had been in harbour at this crucial time. Fisher too was not pleased with the way things had gone and blamed Keyes for the missed chance by the *C9*, although this submarine was not under his orders at the time. It was another stage in the worsening relationship between the two men. Yet the main lesson seems to have been overlooked – there was no laid-down procedure for contacting the submarines on their patrol line once they had parted company with the *Lurcher*.

Sunday 20 December
What a chance we have missed! I hear that the MONARCH sighted their battlecruisers retiring from the coast but of course could not catch them up. I am still wondering why the Admiralty insisted on our being placed off Terschelling. If there is a mousehole in the corner of a room one does not place the mousetrap along one wall, but rather in front of the hole. We all think this should have been done with us around the mouths of the Elbe and Weser rivers.

Within days Cochrane was taking the *E7* to sea again. Admiralty information indicated that the Germans might be intending to carry out a second raid in quick succession. Eight of Commodore Tyrwhitt's destroyers were sent to a position off Terschelling from where they could easily be sent on into the Bight if needs be. Two submarines, the *E2* and *E7*, were sent to keep watch off the German bases for 36 hours from dawn on the 23rd when they were to return. On the 22nd the Admiralty thought that the likelihood of a German sortie was minimal and recalled the destroyers but could not get a signal through to the two submarines, for by then they were outside

84

the reception range of their low-powered sets. The *E2* returned at dusk on the 24th, having seen a few trawlers on patrol and attempted to attack a U-boat. The *E7* stayed longer, Cochrane understanding, incorrectly, that he could remain out for an extra 24 hours, and so spent Christmas near the Weser lightship. In this way they were in position when a fresh attempt was made to launch an attack from the seaplane carriers.

Tuesday 22 December

Was woken and told that the E2 and E7 were going out at once. I turned out thinking it was 6 o'clock and found out it was only 20 minutes after midnight. We got under way at 2 o'clock. Our departure is not as expected from all the rumours of yesterday but of a signal from the Admiralty at midnight.

Apparently their fleet is expected to come out for another raid on the 23rd. If only we can meet them and not have the bad luck E11 had it will be an absolutely glorious Xmas. We all have the feeling that we are going to bring it off. Cochrane has got on his green hat (always lucky I believe) and there is something in the air which seems to spell success, while to look at Cochrane makes anything else seem impossible.

The Admiralty was keen to try and use the seaplane again to raid the Zeppelin sheds near Cuxhaven. Three seaplane carriers, each with three aircraft armed with three 20 lb bombs were detailed for the operation, being escorted by Tyrwhitt's destroyers, while eleven submarines were to cover the operation, including the *E7* which was to be included in the operation by the chance extension of her time on patrol.

Once again the Grand Fleet was to be positioned in the middle of the North Sea in case the actions of the seaplane carriers should lead to the chance of a major fleet action, though, as Keyes commented, since they were 220 miles from Heligoland, this seemed unlikely. Smooth water was essential for the operations of the seaplanes, for without it they could not be hoisted out nor take off, and this too seemed to be an unlikely occurrence in December in the North Sea. However, there was a favourable forecast and the Admiralty gave the go-ahead with Christmas Day for the raid.

Keyes set off from Harwich on the 23rd with his two destroyers *Lurcher* and *Firedrake* shepherding three D, six E class submarines and the *S1*. The three carriers sailed from Harwich on Christmas Eve and were escorted by the destroyers to a position about 12 miles north of Heligoland where the aircraft would start their sorties. After take-off the seaplanes were to fly south to raid the Zeppelin sheds outside Cuxhaven, then, flying westwards to rendezvous again with their carriers, they would take the opportunity to fly over the river estuaries and note the positions of the German fleet.

As the force approached the launch position just before dawn on Christmas Day the planet Venus was seen shining brightly in the east, regarded by many as a good omen for the day's events, a latter-day "Star in the East". But whatever may be thought of such omens it was a perfect day for the airmen with the calm seas and no sign of fog. Even so, of the nine aircraft only seven were able to take off, the other two being hoisted in again. Luck too was with the British force for they had been sighted in the early morning light by the *U6*. Foiled in an attempt to attack a destroyer by a last-minute alteration in course, the submarine waited until the British ships had moved away and then surfaced to report their presence.

Yet planning was faulty, for the exact position of the target near Cuxhaven was not known, the pilots being briefed that the hangars were believed to be at Capelle, a village about five miles south of the port. This information was incorrect and this, coupled with patches of fog, which were met as the aircraft reached the land, meant that only one of the aircraft got anywhere near the target, where under heavy AA fire he jettisoned his bombs without realizing how close he was!

The pilot of another of the seaplanes, having failed to find the target, turned out to sea passing over the sand dunes at only 150 feet, and then began to have trouble with his engine. He actually landed on the sea to make emergency repairs, taxied away from a patrol trawler that got too inquisitive and then took off again for the rendezvous. Petrol shortage forced him down again and he was picked up by the *Lurcher*. A second seaplane dropped his bombs near the cruisers *Stralsund* and *Graudenz*, but they caused no damage. This pilot too was forced down by lack of fuel before reaching the rendezvous and was picked up by one of Tyrwhitt's destroyers. Another aircraft that had to come down on the sea was piloted by Flight-Commander Kilner and carried as the observer Lieutenant Erskine Childers, who before the war had made his name as the author of the thriller *The Riddle of the Sands* which was set in the Frisian Islands over which they now flew.

Flight-Lieutenant Miley found himself with only a few minutes petrol left when he was delighted to see a submarine surface nearby and was able to recognize it as friendly. It was Nasmith in the *E11*. Taking the pilot and his observer on board, Nasmith began to tow the seaplane towards the rendezvous with the waiting carriers. Hardly had they got under way when a Zeppelin was sighted and two other seaplanes came down on the sea nearby. They too were out of fuel. With four more airmen to rescue and all the aircraft to be sunk, as there was now no hope of salvaging them, Nasmith had to race the approaching Zeppelin. To add to his worries another submarine was sighted heading towards the little group. By the time the last of the airmen had clambered aboard and been bundled down below the Zeppelin was nearly overhead and the other submarine must surely have been in a firing position. Nasmith waited no longer and took the *E11* hurriedly to 40 feet. No sooner were they dived when two small bombs were heard to explode seemingly overhead and with an alarming noise.

Leutnant Hirsch, who commanded the airship *L5*, recorded the incident in his patrol report:

> As we approached, the submarine appeared to be taking off the occupants of the aircraft in great haste, and then she dived to avoid us. The seaplanes remained afloat, one being damaged with its tail bent upwards. At the same time we sighted several British cruisers and destroyers on a southerly course (to the north of us). In order to prevent these vessels from picking up the seaplanes and in the hope that we might damage the submarine we dropped two bombs among the seaplanes. They exploded about 30 yards away and we did not observe any effect.

Luckily the other submarine was the *D6* (Lieutenant-Commander R. C. Halahan), who was out of position but had raced towards the stranded seaplanes to see if he could help. As the great airship passed overhead Halahan had prudently dived, unaware of the anxiety that this action was to give to Nasmith. After a while he surfaced near one of the seaplanes to ensure that the pilot was not still aboard only to find that the Zeppelin was less than 100 yards away and very low. Staying on the surface only long enough to confirm that the crew of the seaplane were safe he dived again amid a hail of machine-gun bullets.

The seventh seaplane also came down on the sea. The two airmen sank their machine and were themselves picked up by a Dutch fishing vessel. After being landed in Holland they were returned to Britain as "shipwrecked mariners" rather than being interned. In itself the raid achieved nothing and caused the loss of all the aircraft taking part. Yet these early seaplanes had flown about 120 miles to carry out their mission and had only failed to return to the carriers through a shortage of fuel rather than the actions of the enemy. They had failed to find, let alone bomb, the Zeppelin sheds, but had overflown some units of the German fleet in their anchorages. Their presence was no small surprise to the Germans. Two battlecruisers, the *von der Tann* and the *Moltke*, both took in their anti-torpedo nets and raised steam in anticipation of orders to proceed into the Bight, but despite some stories to the contrary they never even weighed anchor. The Germans too considered it a memorable day for their airmen; both seaplanes and the Zeppelins had carried out valuable reconnaissance while the carrier *Empress* had been bombed, though not hit.

Cochrane, spending his extra day on patrol in the *E7*, was surprised when he surfaced on Christmas morning to find one of the Zeppelins directly overhead, perhaps because the submarine's shape was visible in the calm sea, perhaps for some other reason. Cochrane promptly dived again but for the rest of the morning whenever he put his periscope up the Zeppelin was always near by. Playing safe, the *E7* remained submerged, in ignorance of the events taking place in the area.

Surfaced. Cochrane nipped up to see if any land was in sight and I was standing on the ladder waiting for orders when his face appeared covered with a broad grin, and he sung out for us to dive again. He had gazed around the horizon and seen nothing but some trawlers and then looked up into the sky and almost overhead was a Zeppelin about 600 feet up! We kept at 20 feet while we all had a look at her through the periscope and then went to the bottom. Half an hour later we came back to periscope depth but the Zeppelin was still in sight.

We have been off the mouth of the Elbe all afternoon, I do wish something would come along as a Xmas present. During the afternoon it began to get misty.

At 4 o'clock we surfaced, anchored and began to charge the battery. It was a flat calm sea and a fog as thick as pea soup, we could see about 100 yards. We meant to charge until 7.0 but shortly before then I heard a most extraordinary bellow which was followed by the electric horn and everyone came tumbling down from the bridge. We went straight to the bottom and I heard that a deep and loud siren had sounded just astern of us.

We hoped to hear the anchor cables of the High Seas Fleet rattling down all round us and then when we heard them weighing we should know the fog was lifting and would be able to catch them. When we surfaced the fog was as thick as ever, and not a sound, so weighed the anchor and then dived again. Then we settled down to our Christmas dinner of soup, rabbit pie and plum pudding. We had a gramophone going all evening, some of the new records are very good.

This was a comic way to spend Christmas! We were submerged for 20 hours 51 minutes.

The *S1* making her first patrol in the Heligoland Bight, had a nasty experience. Having reached her patrol area off the Ems, she dived to await the dawn and, hopefully, the enemy. However, at a depth of 30 feet she struck something solid, either a wreck or maybe another submarine (though German records show it was no U-boat) and this knocked off part of her keel. As a consequence she surfaced like a cork, no longer able to dive and an easy prey for any enemy that might be met. Like the *Archimede* a few days earlier, she saw no sign of the enemy during her long trip back to Harwich, where she was anxiously awaited. For, by that time the *D8* had passed through her area and had seen a large patch of oil which even then was still bubbling to the surface. Her report of this had raised fears for the *S1's* safety.

The *S1* was not the only boat whose return was a matter of concern. Cochrane, by staying out the extra day, was overdue when he returned at noon on the 27th. Their passage back had not been pleasant for the good weather of Christmas morning had been followed by the fog which Hallifax recorded in his diary, and this had been followed by stormy winds and pouring rain.

Boxing Day

Surfaced at 1.15 am and went ahead on the engines at 10½ knots as all the fog had gone. Sea very phosphorescent so we dived again until we passed the island. Wind freshened from the south during the forenoon but it had been delightfully fine. By 10 o'clock it had started to cloud over and was blowing quite hard. When we altered course for the North Hinder it brought the sea on to the port bow and made it pretty wet on the bridge. During the afternoon the sea got up a lot more and after dark Cochrane came down from the bridge. He said that it was raining so hard that no one could see 100 yards so it was useless having anyone up there.

27 December

Pushed on into Harwich. It was blowing like nothing on earth and raining cats and dogs. Got alongside at 11.30 am and found all the boats but E15 in, the E2 being the inner boat, which looked as if the rest had been out as well. When I got to the Wardroom I found that we had been given up for lost, the E2 having returned on Christmas morning. The Commodore had learnt that mines had been laid off the Jade river and feared we had gone up on one of them.

So 1914 came to an end. The Christmas Day seaplane raid and supporting operations had done little but show the potential of the new Royal Navy Air Service, although it did show the strength of the Royal Navy's position in the North Sea in that they could carry out such a raid without hindrance. These naval operations on Christmas Day did, however, contrast strongly with the Western Front where the soldiers involved in the bloody fighting of the previous four months suddenly engaged in a spontaneous but unofficial truce. At sea five months of war had not produced a second Trafalgar, indeed the Navy's shortcomings had highlighted its inability to deliver the crucial blows to the High Seas Fleet whenever it had put to sea. The submariners had had a frustrating time with so many incidents foiled by faulty torpedoes or more simply by not being in the right place at the right time. The E7 had shared these frustrations with her sister boats as well as suffering the traumas of defects and the necessity to change commanding officers. It was to be hoped that the fortunes of 1915 would be different.

7

1915: A New Year

THE NEW YEAR was just two hours old when a U-boat demonstrated once again that the submarine was a weapon to be feared and gave Jellicoe more concern for the safety of the Grand Fleet. This new misfortune was to take place in what was thought to be the safety of the English Channel midway between Portland Bill and Start Point, and at a time when the Navy was still smarting from its inability to intercept the German raids on the east coast.

On 22 December Korvettenkapitän Schneider took the *U24* from the Ems down the Dutch coast to Zeebrugge and then on up the canal to Bruges where he arrived on Christmas Eve. At Bruges the Germans were establishing an advanced base for their submarines to operate against Allied shipping both on the cross-Channel routes to France or further west in the Channel where the ships were forced by geography into a comparatively small area at the end of their trans-Atlantic voyage. On 27 December Schneider sailed again to operate off Plymouth. In the Straits of Dover he was worried more by the bad weather than the Anglo-French patrols which in any case had been weakened by defects. At midnight on 29/30 December, when just south of the Isle of Wight, he sighted two unescorted battleships of the 6th Battle Squadron heading east for Sheerness, but he did not attack.

From Sheerness came the 5th Battle Squadron to carry out much-needed gunnery training in what was regarded as "safe waters". All day on the 31st the eight battleships with only two old destroyers in attendance carried out their exercises, and for four hours Schneider tried to manoeuvre to attack them, but without success. With his batteries nearly flat and the British ships seemingly steaming towards Portsmouth Schneider withdrew to charge. To his surprise and delight just after 1 o'clock on New Year's morning he sighted three large and darkened ships coming towards his position. Eventually he fired a single torpedo at the third ship in the line, HMS *Queen* at a range of only 750 yards and missed. However, he had not been seen and the remaining five ships of Vice-Admiral Sir Lewis Bayly's squadron were then sighted. Again, with the last ship of the line as his target, Schneider fired two torpedoes, one of which struck HMS *Formidable*. An hour later, having taken the *U24* around the other side of the squadron he fired another torpedo which also hit the great ship. Another hour later and the *Formidable* had gone to the bottom. German submarines had scored another triumph even when it is realized that the battleships were virtually unescorted, for the destroyers were a mile astern, were only two cables apart, were steering a steady course and making good only ten knots. Truly all the ingredients of a submariner's dream! So, despite Jellicoe's expressed fears of the effects of submarine attack which he had held since the beginning of the war, this incident showed how little some Admirals had learned from Weddigen or Horton.

For the British submariners at Harwich the year opened in a less spectacular manner. Some boats were sent up into the Bight for what might be called routine patrols; the weather was bad, they saw little of the enemy and made no attacks. In Harwich there were rumours of "stunts" while Commanding Officers like Cochrane tried to dream up schemes for using their craft in a more useful manner. These never came to reality.

12 January

(I found) Cochrane examining the charts of the Jade and Weser rivers during the forenoon – he evidently intends to try at the Schilling Roads at the first opportunity. There are only two channels by which we might go in, but I should not be surprised if the Germans use only one and have mined the other. But, which is which? It will be hard to get in if the buoys are not there for I think we must try at night. The land is low and flat and it is hard to distinguish landmarks. There are any amount of sandbanks, and of course currents. If we do get in and do anything it will be harder to get out!

At lunch Twyman came up and said "Further developments". He had just been told by Jefferies (RNR Sub-Lieutenant and Third Hand of the E6) that he is coming on a stunt with us and also Erskine Childers. He knows all that coast and will be invaluable. Apparently there will be some work in the Berthon boat [small collapsable boat carried by submarines]. It is going to be great fun. Still, I hope that the wind goes down a bit.

Lieutenant Erskine Childers RNVR was one of those larger than life characters that wars bring to the fore. When he offered his services to the Admiralty at the beginning of the war he was already more experienced and older than his contempories in rank, having served as an artilleryman in the Boer War, but because of his unique qualifications the Admiralty had no doubts about accepting him. He was the son of an earlier First Lord of the Admiralty, he had been a Clerk to the House of Commons and, more important, he was a keen yachtsman. His passion for sailing had meant many summers spent sailing around the islands and along the coast between the Elbe and Borkum, and the knowledge thus acquired was put to good use in writing a very successful novel, *The Riddle of the Sands*, which was published in 1903 and depicted a German attempt to invade Britain. He had already flown over this coast while taking part in the Christmas Day air raid on Cuxhaven. Now it was proposed to exploit his intimate knowledge of the area in another operation, although the Admiralty were completely unaware that only weeks before the outbreak of war he had used his yacht in a clandestine operation smuggling German arms into Ireland. After the war Childers embraced the cause of the Irish rebels not recognizing the treaty that brought into existence the Irish Free State. In November, 1922, he was arrested by the Free State forces, court-martialled and shot, his name branded as a traitor by both English and Irish, a victim of his conscience and the politics of the times. Tantalizingly, Hallifax's diary is the only reference to such a proposed operation by the E7 in the early days of January, 1915, and the patrol does not seem to have been carried out.

A sweep was carried out by Tyrwhitt's forces, three light cruisers and thirty-three destroyers, supported by Beatty's battlecruisers in the area between Borkum and the Horn Reef on 19 January. Three submarines, the *E5, E10* and *E15*, were stationed in the Bight during this operation which replaced yet another seaplane raid abandoned because of expected bad weather. The force left Harwich in a heavy snowstorm, while in the Bight the snow cleared, leaving the ships and submarines to face the misery of near-gale-force winds and freezing temperatures. Sadly, nothing more was ever heard of the *E10*, and it is presumed that she became one more victim of the many mines in the area.

The next moves came, once again, as a result of the Admiralty becoming aware that the Germans intended another operation into the North Sea. Such a move was indeed planned, one similar to that of the British only a few days earlier. The German 1st and 2nd Scouting Groups, three battlecruisers, a heavy cruiser, four light cruisers and twenty-two destroyers were ordered out towards the Dogger Bank to gain intelligence of any British patrols met and to destroy the fishing fleet. The German move was timed in the hope that the British would be caught in harbour still refuelling after their own sortie.

Nevertheless, both Beatty and Tyrwhitt were ordered to sea and given a rendezvous only 180 miles from Heligoland at 7 am on the 24th. Keyes was ordered to take his two destroyers and four submarines towards Borkum and, showing that something at least had been learnt from past mistakes, he was warned to keep within signalling range for any change in orders.

Ever hopeful for good weather, even in January, Keyes had already sailed on the morning of the 23rd from Harwich in support of an anticipated seaplane raid. The *Lurcher*, with the submarines, had to be recalled, so it was after 4 o'clock in the afternoon before Keyes got his new orders and set out once more with the submarines across the North Sea. By then there was thick fog in the harbour and, with all Tyrwhitt's destroyers trying to leave as well, it was fortunate that there were no accidents. Because of the delay it was impossible that the submarines would reach a position where they could hope to attack the enemy should he return before dark on the 24th. They were therefore given new positions off Norderney and Heligoland where they could make contact if the Germans were delayed returning until the morning of the 25th. In any case the four submarines were instructed to return on the evening of the 25th, or earlier in the event of bad weather.

Saturday 23 January

At 10.50 am we and the E4 were told to get ready to shove off and we left 30 minutes later. We had barely gone a hundred yards when the MAIDSTONE signalled "Return". We dashed after the E4 and caught her at the entrance, and then back we came. When opposite the ship she signalled "What have you come back for? Proceed with all despatch". So off we went again! At 2.15 pm the E4 who was on W/T watch turned about and signalled "Return to harbour". The sky was looking very threatening and we thought it looked bad for the seaplanes and assumed that the stunt had been postponed. Got in at 4.30 and made fast outside the E4 on the PANDORA. Cochrane told me to keep everything ready for shoving off.

Very foggy in the harbour and by the time we shoved off again it was dark as well. The LURCHER, FIREDRAKE with E4, E7, E8 and E11 left in a bunch and barged through the fog somehow. When beyond the CORK lightship the fog lifted and we found the FIREDRAKE ahead and no-one else in sight! Had we gone on earlier we should have been half way up the Dutch coast by now. It's quite calm and a good moon. Not very cold, but it will be if the wind rises.

While the submarines spent most of the 24th trying to reach their positions off Norderney or Heligoland the rival fleets met in what is now known as the Battle of the Dogger Bank. Initially it was a day that seemed about to give the Royal Navy the crushing victory over the Germans that they so desperately sought. With the enemy heading at full speed back towards their bases the *Seydlitz*, Admiral Hipper's flagship, was badly hit aft, the two after-turrets being put out of action by a fierce fire which necessitated flooding her magazines. The heavy cruiser *Blücher* was also badly hit. At this crucial stage Beatty's flagship, *HMS Lion*, was hit, though fortunately with few casualties, but nevertheless began to loose speed and had to pull out of the line. Having just made a large alteration of course to avoid a submarine, although in fact there was no U-boat within 60 miles, Beatty lost control of the battle. Aided by poor signalling and a less than vigorous pursuit by Beatty's deputy, the enemy was allowed to escape while the unfortunate *Blücher* was pounded until she capsized and sank. As for the *Lion* she was towed back to Rosyth.

24 January

Apparently another raid is expected today and we are to catch the ships returning, our position to be between Heligoland and the Weser.

After diving for a trim at 7 o'clock we surfaced and I went on watch. It was beastly cold with the bridge screen furled and the boat has no warmth inside. At 8.30 saw some black shapes coming up on us so we dived. They were destroyers, probably ours, but we did not want to give the show away by challenging them. It was annoying as we had no time to waste if we were to be in position by morning. When we surfaced we found a valve had been left open on diving and we had flooded the engines. It took some time to drain them down and in starting too early there were awful bumps and noises. Number 3 piston and connecting rod had broken on the starboard engine, we had to sling the piston and disconnect the rod. Cochrane took it very quietly.

25 January

At 1.30 this morning we could see lights in the sky to the eastward which Cochrane took to be the searchlights on Heligoland. At 3.40 I went on watch as Cochrane had been up all night. It was inky black and so cold and dismal standing on the bridge in solitary grandeur waiting for the High Seas Fleet to come in range. We had all tubes ready, with a hand standing by each one. Cochrane relieved me again at 6 o'clock and after drinking some cocoa I turned in. I have ceased to care about keeping the blankets clean and now get between them, clothes or no clothes. The boat is freezing cold; the air is raw and damp and I can't get warm in spite of the leather waistcoat and sweater, now covered by an additional Navy League sweater.

As they expected, the submarines were too late. The Germans had slipped back into harbour before they were in position; in fact the lights on Heligoland seen by Cochrane were lit to aid the return of the Fleet. Only the *E8* to the north-west of Heligoland saw anything of the enemy and was able to fire at a destroyer flotilla. The torpedo, set to run at a depth of only six feet, must have been sighted, as the destroyers scattered like a flock of partridges and disappeared from sight at high speed.

25 January

We dived at 7.30 this morning and were dived all day. We sighted nothing but some minesweeping trawlers. We surfaced again at 6.30 and directly the hatch was opened the air turned blue and misty, but almost immediately we noticed the fresh air entering the boat and my teeth stopped chattering. We got under way on the engines and headed for Harwich.

The *E7* returned to Harwich on the evening of the 26th to hear the results of the battle as they were then known, while the engineers began to work to repair the damaged engine.

As far as this particular battle is concerned it remains only to comment on one signal made during the battle. At the height of the action Rear Admiral Sir Archibald Moore, at that time commanding

96

the battlecruisers in the absence of Beatty in the damaged *Lion*, signalled that he was retiring, as Commodore (S) had reported that the whole of the High Seas Fleet was at sea. Keyes had made no such signal, and when a copy of Moore's signal was shown to him during a visit to the Admiralty he protested most strongly to this effect. But Fisher had already heard of the signal and blamed Keyes for the misinformation that was partly responsible for Moore's failure to follow up the initial successes of the day. In view of Fisher's continuing hostility, Keyes decided to ask Winston Churchill, as First Lord, if he could be found employment elsewhere. He hated to leave the Submarine Service but it seemed a necessary course of action and would be the best for all concerned. Churchill reluctantly agreed. There the matter rested until 8 February when Keyes was suddenly ordered to report to the Admiralty where he was told that he was to leave the following morning to go to the Mediterranean, there to become the Chief of Staff to Rear Admiral Carden who was to command the Allied Squadron charged with forcing a passage of the Dardanelles to Constantinople. There was so little time before Keyes left England that he was never to return to Harwich. The unnecessary haste left a nasty taste behind.

4 February
I heard this morning that the Commodore is going to sea, I suppose he is getting one of the new battleships. He must be pretty fed up with the Admiralty by this time and I don't wonder that he wants to get out of it, especially as it is said that Fisher dislikes him and has been trying to find an excuse to get rid of him.

6 February
Heard a rumour today that the Commodore is going to be put on half-pay instead of going to a new battleship. An infernal shame if true. Hall is to be the new Commodore. He will be in the Admiralty and not here at Harwich. From what I hear he takes no interest in anything and dislikes Keyes and also tries to crab anything of his, so it is not a pleasant outlook for the submarine service. The very idea of personal likes, and dislikes especially, coming to play in wartime, without regard for the interests of the service, makes me furious.

Keyes' sudden departure meant the return of Sydney Stewart Hall as Commodore (S), the man who had held the post from 1910 to 1912 and had himself been relieved by Keyes. Hall was well known to the

First Sea Lord, having been the Secretary to Lord Fisher's Royal Commission on Oil Fuel and Engines for which he was made a CB in the New Year's Honours List in 1914. With Fisher's return to the Admiralty after the outbreak of war Hall was brought from the command of *HMS Roxburgh*, a light cruiser with the Grand Fleet, to the Admiralty, there to be an additional Naval Assistant to the First Sea Lord with particular emphasis on submarine matters. While this may reflect Fisher's own keen interest in submarines, it also adds weight to the conjecture that Fisher always had him in mind for the post of Commodore (S) to relieve Keyes, for Hall's post in the First Sea Lord's office was not filled when he left. It is perhaps for these reasons that his return was regarded with suspicion by many serving submariners. Nevertheless he was an officer of rare technical and administrative ability, combining his extensive technical knowledge with a practical seaman's outlook to an unusual degree in those days. With his even temperment he tended to work quietly and modestly providing continual encouragement for all his submariners. Yet the nature of the appointment was also changed, with Commodore (S) more involved with administration and training, leaving Captain Waistell of the *Maidstone* to operate the flotilla at Harwich as ordered directly by the Admiralty.

Hall was to remain as Commodore (S) for the remainder of the war, his only reward being promotion to Rear Admiral while the honours and decorations went elsewhere. Despite Hall's undoubted ability and long tenure of office, it was Keyes who held the affection and loyalty of the submariners of those days, and even today is the better remembered.

Keyes was not the only commander to go after the Battle of the Dogger Bank, which was the highwater mark of German naval activity in the North Sea for the early period of the war, being the last of the battlecruiser raids. They had achieved little, had failed disastrously to bring any part of the Grand Fleet to battle on terms favourable to the Germans and had suffered more than the British. They had been truly fortunate not to have suffered even more severely. It cost Admiral Von Ingenohl his position as Commander-in-Chief of the High Seas Fleet and his successor, Admiral von Pohl, was given less freedom of action by the Kaiser.

In the months that followed, the pattern of operations for the British was constantly dictated by fears of further raids into the North Sea by the High Seas Fleet. In reality it became a war of small ships

8.   HMS *Adamant* at Mudros with E-class submarine alongside.

9.   Sub-Lieutenant Twyman with the 12-pdr 8-cwt gun fitted on the aftercasing of the *E7*.

10. HMS *E7* alongside the aircraft carrier *Ben-my-Chree* at Mudros 3 September, 1915, with one of the carrier's Sopwith Schneider seaplanes resting on the forecasing.

11. HMS *E7* at Kephalo Bay shortly before sailing for her last patrol. The monitor in the background is probably HMS *Abercrombie*.

12. Stern section of the German submarine *UB7* still on the railway truck which had brought it from Germany to Pola for reassembly.

13. Stern section of the *UB7* being positioned by crane in a floating dock for reassembly.

14. Interior of an E-Class submarine – the fore-ends showing the rear doors of the forward torpedo tubes.

15. Interior of HMS *E41* – the engine room.

with minelayers and minesweepers on both sides becoming increasingly active. The U-boats roamed further afield in increasing numbers while the British submarines kept their watch in the Heligoland Bight, and of course the ever-active Tyrwhitt kept his forces constantly alert to watch for any movement by the enemy. Anti-submarine tactics on both sides depended on luck; there was no way of detecting a submerged submarine, while attacking one was limited to gunfire against any part that could be seen, and the top of a periscope is a small enough target. In the last resort there was ramming, but this could lead to as much damage to the attacking ship as to the submarine.

In addition to routine patrols by single submarines, Captain Waistell was required to react to information received by the Admiralty of possible enemy movements. Such an event occurred in early February when the *E5*, *E11* and *E12* were sent out to cover the expected movement of a squadron of battleships from the Elbe to the Jade. The *E5* managed to get as far as Heligoland before some of the worst weather of the winter forced her to return, while the *E12* was forced back when she had only reached a position off Terschelling.

The third submarine, the *E11*, grounded on a shoal outside Yarmouth and remained there for three hours before getting off on the rising tide and struggling on to reach her allotted position off the Elbe. It was the sort of weather that Nasmith's two colleagues, Commanders Laurence and Horton, were experiencing in the Baltic. An easterly gale caught any spray and flung it over the bridge to freeze on anything solid and add to the sodden misery of the watchkeepers. Around the conning-tower hatch the ice had to be scraped away continuously to ensure that the hatch could be shut if necessary. Nasmith and his crew kept their watch, exposed to the cruelty of the elements by night, and for a day and a half tried to remain dived in the estuary where the varying densities of fresh and salt water added to the difficulties of trimming the submarine in the gale-swept waters. Then they fought their way home again.

The *E13*, Lieutenant-Commander G. Layton, also went out in these awful conditions but remained only six hours off the Maas light vessel before turning back. To add insult to the injury of the weather conditions, she was then mistaken for a U-boat by the Great Eastern Railway steamer *Colchester* who attempted to ram her.

Submarines at sea tend to be no man's friend and stories of "own goals" involving submarines are legion in all navies, not only in the

Great War but ever since. Luckily such incidents usually come to nought and are most marked by the righteous indignation of the submariners involved. Soon after the *E13's* encounter with the *Colchester* the *E14* was involved in a similar meeting with some of Tyrwhitt's destroyers, and, not for the first time for one of the Harwich submarines it would seem, judging from Hallifax's account of the meeting.

> ... told me about the AURORA and four destroyers attacking them. The E14 was broadside on so they must have had a good view of her, but the destroyers rushed towards and opened fire. Not a single shot fell within 100 yards! Boyle saw the skipper of one of the destroyers the next day who told him that they noticed the submarine had a straight upper deck but thought that she MIGHT be German! In spite of this when they sighted her again after dark and reported to the AURORA they were told to go back and sink her. They went back but could not find the E14 again. It would be a jolly good thing if one of us were to let fly a fish at them when they behave like this, they are absolutely irresponsible.

The *E7* spent most of the month of March at Ipswich in dock returning just in time for a visit from His Majesty the King to the base to see the submarines and destroyers. However, even kings have to play second fiddle to the requirements of their forces in war and he arrived at Harwich to find the base almost empty of destroyers. The weather suddenly looked promising for yet another attempt to carry out one of the seaplane raids and Tyrwhitt had taken most of his force to sea. For Tyrwhitt it meant that the King could not present him with the CB which he had been awarded for his part in the battle of the previous August and had never been able to go to the Palace to receive. Undeterred, the King took the opportunity to visit the submarines, minesweepers and various other craft which now thronged the port which only a short time previously had been concerned only with railway ferries to Holland.

Thursday 25 March

Left Ipswich just before 6 o'clock. Found on arrival that the King was expected in the forenoon with Divisions at 10.30. Uniform for officers was monkey jackets with greatcoats, the men were in number 5's. Poor chaps they were nearly frozen. HM arrived just after 11 o'clock and walked down the front rank (E7 and E8 crews) then passed the ship's company of the MAIDSTONE. From there he went over the E16, Talbot's new boat. After that he went to the DIDO [an old cruiser serving as an accommodation ship for the destroyer flotillas] which is alongside the jetty, and the boats' crews manned their boats, falling in on the casings. HM then came back past us and got into a motor boat and went back up harbour being cheered by us as he went.

One of the few submarines that was at sea during this visit was the *D1*, Cochrane's old boat, now commanded by Lieutenant E. W. B. Ryan. She was on patrol off the Ems and in thick fog was passed by a U-boat which appeared suddenly from out of the murk only about 40 yards off. Showing remarkable speed of reaction the German loosed off several rounds from a rifle which went harmlessly overhead before both submarines lost each other in the fog. It was an incident which caused Hallifax to remark that he was resolved in future to keep a loaded pistol with him when on watch.

The *E7* was the next to go on patrol into the Bight and she left Harwich on the last day of March, her first operational time at sea for two months. She was off Heligoland between dawn on 2 April till dusk on the 4th, on one occasion in the fog coming to within 1½ miles of the island fortress. She fired a torpedo at a trawler and, not surprisingly, missed. What she had also missed was a brief training cruise by the High Seas Fleet on 29 March when they reached as far west as Norderney before returning to reach the Jade the following morning. Apart from the fact that this was the first time that Admiral von Pohl had taken his fleet to sea it was historic in that three airships were airborne and being used to scout for the fleet.

1 April

Kept watch from 0.30 to 2.30 this morning. A lovely night with a bright full moon and not cold as the wind was nearly astern. We stood up from the Hinder to the latitude of Heligoland and then altered to the east by which time it was a beautifully warm spring day. I feel so full of optimism. I have each time, but this time especially so. With this bright moon at nights it will be difficult to charge the batteries each night and we shall have to conserve them as much as possible.

2 April. (Good Friday)

At least one trawler in sight all day. Beastly cold in the boat but the "Jaeger" combinations supplied with the oilskin overalls are lovely things.

3 April

At 1.0 pm we came up to 21 feet and saw a German merchant ship and reluctantly Cochrane decided to let her go. Then later when he was looking round he sighted something astern and ordered "Get the stern tube ready, quick." [The operation took longer than usual and then because of a confusion of orders Cochrane missed the chance to fire.] He was absolutely furious and miserable at having missed firing at a target upon which he had had sights for about two minutes. I could have burst into tears when he told me. Fritz was stopped about 300 yards astern of us, guns up and flags flying. Poor Cochrane is heartbroken at missing this chance and I am miserable for I know that he blames me but try as I do I can't really blame myself. If anyone in the flotilla deserved good luck it is Cochrane. What a horrible day this has been after all my earlier optimism, I wish that I could undo it all or wake up and find it all a dream.

4 April

On the surface: damp drifting fog, visibility about 100 yards at the most, wind falling. We dived at 10.30 am and have been cruising around on one motor wondering just where we are! C said at lunch that he wondered if we could say the fog was too thick and stay an extra day, but no, it won't do. Just before 3 o'clock the fog lifted a bit and C saw an armed trawler and told me to get the starboard tube ready at once. Everything seemed to go well, but. . . .

There followed another of those incidents which dogged Cochrane's efforts to make his first successful attack on the enemy, incidents which partially reflect the general state of efficiency of the crew under Feilmann which Cochrane had yet to change totally, and also the consequent lack of experience of Hallifax. This time it was a material failure of the firing mechanism of the torpedoes, as a modification had not been carried out. It was one of those things which everyone else in the flotilla knew about – even Petty Officer Sims, the rating responsible for the torpedoes and their tubes, but which had never been officially publicized and therefore not carried out in the *E7*. Luckily they had another chance at the same trawler and the torpedo ran straight and true, but with her shallow draft the target was unharmed. Even so, 'Cochrane quite bucked up after getting it off'.

It was a disappointing patrol for Cochrane, leaving him frustrated by the inability to make one attack and missing another after a second drill failure, while realizing that his First Lieutenant, for whatever reason, did not entirely match his own standards. The patrol is of interest too in noting the amount of time that the *E7* spent dived, an average of 20 hours a day. Such a figure would have been regarded as highly unusual in August, 1914, but now, only eight months later, it passes without comment in Hallifax's diary.

These long periods submerged were a great strain on the submarine's battery and every effort was made to economize in the use of battery power including sitting stopped on the bottom for long periods. Hot meals during the day were out of the question in these conditions and the crew took to having a hearty meal at night while on the surface charging the battery. The Admiralty acknowledged the unsatisfactory nature of this state of affairs with the issue of "Extra Special Emergency Comforts", or as they became more simply known "Submarine Comforts". These were additional rations designed not only to increase the amount of food available but also to add some variety and by including items like bottled fruit to stimulate jaded palates. Boredom was another enemy.

Friday 23 April
   The day dragged most horribly slowly. Fortunately I brought a good long book out with me and it ought to last till tomorrow night. By teatime C had read the New Magazine right through, advertisements and all, and took to playing patience. Twyman has slept nearly the whole day and when awake dips into my book whenever I go to the periscope. We have had a few turns on the gramophone which made a pleasant change. Never a sight of a vessel all day.

The beginning of May saw five submarines involved in another stunt with one of the seaplane carriers. However, the operation was memorable not so much for the aircraft's activities, or lack of them, but for the submarines' encounter with a Zeppelin. Five submarines were on their way to their positions off the German coast when the airship approached them and all immediately dived, with the exception of the *E5*. As his was the only boat fitted with a gun, Benning tried to get in a shot but the airship came in so fast that the gun was soon at maximum elevation without even getting one shot off, so Benning followed his friends and dived. Lieutenant-Commander Layton was convinced that four bombs exploded quite close to the *E13*, making a terrific noise and shaking everything up. Benning thought that he too was bombed, as did Lieutenant-Commander Moncrieffe in the *D4*. Benning came to the surface again a little distance from where he had dived and managed to get in three quick shots at the Zeppelin which was hovering over the spot where it had just bombed the *D4*. Benning's crew were convinced that they had scored one hit and were furious that it had not ignited the hydrogen in the airship's envelope. Korvettenkapitän Mathy in the Zeppelin *L9* reported that the shells all fell short and that he was not hit, but for his part claimed to have sunk a submarine, probably the *D4*, and perhaps one other. Moncrieffe's own report of the affair adds some justification to Mathy's claim.

> Five bombs exploded in rapid succession from port bow to starboard quarter; three to port and two to starboard. Boat's depth 29, 31, 34, 37 and 40 feet. The third bomb appeared to be very close and shook everything severely in the boat. Some rivets started in the conning tower casing portside and on the after firing tank. Small loose objects were jumped off tables etc and a layer of dust and paint chips were scattered everywhere.

A week later the *E7* was involved in a similar incident with the same airship, having sailed with the *E5*, *E6*, *E13* and *D1* to take part in what was to be the last attempt to use the seaplane carriers for some time. As was so often the case the raid was abortive due to weather conditions and it is strange to reflect that, having tried, and failed, so often during the winter months, the Admiralty should choose the beginning of summer to take the carriers away for refit and modification. On this occasion the *D1* was damaged by striking a wreck and took no further part, but the remaining four boats were found by the *L9* which forced them to submerge and bombed them. Again, neither side did any damage.

The *E6*, with the *E7* in company, was the first to sight the Zeppelin, which was then many miles away, but the two boats immediately altered course to join up with the other two. By this time the *E7* was the only boat not to have a gun, though Hallifax took the precaution of getting some rifles on to the bridge, later admitting, 'I don't suppose for one moment I hit her but it was a great satisfaction to ease off at her and hope to pick off one of the crew.' Sure enough, the airship closed the group, seeming at first to pass right over the *E7*, but at the last minute altered to pass between the *E6* and *E7*, who were only about 100 yards apart, giving just enough aim-off to allow for the submarines' speed, or so it seemed to those watching anxiously on the bridge with Cochrane. In fact five bombs fell neatly between the two submarines, and then the airships turned to attack the other two submarines while Hallifax marvelled at the ease with which the great craft could be manoeuvred.

> Before she was round, however, the E13 was under, the E5 nearly under and ahead of us the E6 was going down too. There we were, the only boat without a gun, still plodding along. When all three were dived C said we would dive so down we all tumbled – there were about a dozen of us on the bridge all sightseeing! We seemed to take an age to get under and I think everyone was expecting to hear the bombs explode at any moment. Sure enough on our way down to 60 feet we heard three bombs explode.

To the crew of the *E7* it seemed typical of Cochrane that their boat, though having no gun, was the last to dive. In fact Cochrane was furious with the Commanding Officers of the other three boats for diving as he was of the opinion that it was unnecessary provided they all zig-zagged. If there was any wind, that made it that much harder for the Zeppelin to cope with the course changes of the submarines. He also felt that, though the boats should give each other mutual support with their guns, they were much too close together on this occasion. Luckily there was no damage to any of the submarines but one man in the *E6* was wounded by a splinter.

At this stage it is worth recording that in May of the following year a submarine, HMS *E31*, had a very different encounter with a Zeppelin. At that time the *E31* was commanded by Ferdie Feilman and met the *L7* which was returning from a patrol over the North Sea and had been damaged by gunfire from ships of Tyrwhitt's force. By the time the *E31* met with her the great airship was low enough over the sea to be engaged by the submarine's 12-pounder gun. Feilman's gunners opened fire at 4,000 yards and soon obtained three hits. The Zeppelin burst into flames and crashed in under half a minute. The *E31* picked up seven survivors.

Cochrane's views on the defence of a group of submarines against a Zeppelin were to be mirrored nearly thirty years later though then the roles would be reversed with German U-boats seeking mutual protection from Allied aircraft. Setting out from their Biscayan bases to attack Allied convoys during the Battle of the Atlantic they tried the tactic of sailing in groups to give each other protection from marauding aircraft. Increasingly their armament was augmented until by late 1942 boats were going to sea with a 37mm and eight 20mm guns in two quadruple mounts abaft the conning tower, and with as many as four boats travelling together to give the support to each other that they felt was needed.

By this time the Dardanelles campaign was in full swing; troops had landed on the Gallipoli Peninsula and three submarines, the *E11*, *E14* and *E15*, with their depot ship HMS *Adamant*, had already left Harwich to reinforce the elderly B-class submarines in the Mediterranean. Like the submarines sent to the Baltic in October, 1914, no warning was given to enable them to prepare for such an arduous enterprise. Incredible as it may seem today, this 'instant deployment' was to be repeated again as the *E7*, with the *E12* (Lieutenant-Commander K. Bruce) in company, was ordered to the Mediterranean.

Friday 28 May

At 10.45 pm I heard that Cochrane had been sent for by the Captain, while Chamberlain [the First Lieutenant of the MAIDSTONE] told me that two out of the E7, E8 and E12 were going to the Dardanelles. Cochrane came out and after a time I saw him and he told me that we would leave next morning at 9 or 10 o'clock, but I was not to say anything about it that night. The E12, then at Yarmouth, was to be the other boat. Got hold of Twyman who came along to my cabin where we discussed how to get hold of our white uniforms from Gieves, and what to take. Turned in about midnight too excited to sleep

29 May

Had a very busy time from 4.45 onwards. The E12 arrived from Yarmouth about 8 o'clock and had to rush about to some tune. Sailed at 1.0 pm with the E12 and LURCHER for Devonport. It gave promise of a dirty night, the wind in the Channel being south-west.

So the *E7* and her crew left the base at Harwich for the Mediterranean, left the mines, bad weather and boredom of the Heligoland Bight for the unknown tempo of war in the Mediterranean. Worst of all they left still without the satisfaction of seeing one of their torpedoes hit the enemy. It is small wonder that Hallifax's diary is brief for the 29th; there were a hundred and one different jobs requiring his attention as the crew rushed to embark all the stores, fuel and kit required. The marvel is that either boat was ready to sail when it did.

8

The Dardanelles – The Beginnings

AT THE END of July, 1914, the British fleet in the Mediterranean, under the command of Admiral Sir Archibald Berkeley Milne, consisted of one squadron each of battlecruisers, armoured cruisers and light cruisers and a flotilla of sixteen destroyers. In addition there were six obsolete B-class submarines, three stationed at Malta and three at Gibraltar. The French Navy was much stronger in numbers, though many of the ships were not modern. One of the newly completed battleships, the *Jean Bart*, had been detached for special duties and was even then hurrying back to her station from the Baltic where she had been carrying the President on a visit to the Tsar of Russia. A sister ship, the *Courbet*, flew the flag of the French Commander-in-Chief, Vice-Admiral Boué de Lapeyrère.

Of possible enemies the fleet of Austria-Hungary was the more powerful, while that of Turkey was considered to pose little threat despite the efforts of the British Naval Mission in Constantinople over a number of years. The major worry for the British and French was how the Italians would react to the crisis. Since 1882 Italy had been a partner in a Triple Alliance with Germany and Austria-Hungary, though her relations with the Austrians had never been particularly friendly and she was anxious to gain parts of Austrian territory which she regarded as rightfully hers. Nevertheless, in the event of war it was essential for the British and French that Italy should at least remain neutral; her fleet allied to that of the Austrians would put the Allies in a numerically inferior position.

The Germans had only two ships in the area, the battlecruiser *Goeben* and the light cruiser *Breslau*, the squadron being under the able command of Kontreadmiral (Rear Admiral) Wilhelm Souchon. Though only two in number they were to play a part in the opening days of the war that far exceeded their numerical strength. The German ships had been sent to the Mediterranean at the end of 1912 when it was decided that an international squadron should go to Constantinople, then under threat from an advancing Bulgar army. Both ships had been on sea trials after building when the Kaiser had insisted that Germany be represented in the squadron, and they remained in the Mediterranean as a visible sign of the growing power of the Imperial German navy, though the crisis at Constantinople was long since over. There were plans for the *Goeben* to be relieved in October, 1914, by her sister ship, the *Moltke*, but before sailing for home she had to have some 4,000 boiler tubes replaced. The crisis that followed the murders at Sarajevo caught her in the Austrian dockyard at Pola, and it was not before the end of July that she was again ready for sea.

The summer of 1914 found the *Breslau* part of yet another international squadron, this time off the Albanian port of Durazzo. At a nearby anchor berth was the British cruiser, HMS *Defence*. The British ship sailed from the area on 28 July after the Admiralty had issued their Warning Telegram. The *Breslau* sailed three days later under orders from Souchon to meet with the *Goeben*.

Since this is a story of submarines and submariners mention must be made of a young Leutnant serving in the *Breslau* as the Signals Officer, Karl Doenitz. He left the cruiser later in the war to become a submariner and on 4 October, 1918, he was commanding the *UB68* when she was sunk off Malta while attacking a merchant ship. His subsequent career is well known.

Two days before Britain declared war on Germany, on 2 August, the Turks and the Germans signed a secret treaty of alliance. Although primarily aimed at Russia which would thereby be isolated from her princip 1 European ally, France, such a pact was seen by the Germans to have much wider potential in the increasingly critical situation. With the signing of this treaty Berlin immediately ordered the two warships to proceed to Constantinople. That Souchon was able to carry out this order and take his two ships to safety is outside the scope of this story but nevertheless it was a humiliating start to the war in the Mediterranean for the Royal Navy. Escaping the hesitant moves of the British ships, the two German vessels easily reached Turkish waters on 10 August when their crews and the ships themselves nominally became part of the Turkish Navy.

After the débâcles of the Balkan Wars the Turks took a keen interest in the building of two new battleships in England which became a symbol of a new nationalism. The ships, which had been ordered in 1911, had been paid for largely by private money donated by Turks in all walks of life and in July, 1914, the first of the two, named *Sultan Osman I*, was nearly complete and some 500 Turkish officers and men were standing by ready to take her back to Turkey. The second ship, *Sultan Mehmet Rechad V*, was also nearly complete. However, with the European crisis so rapidly heading towards war, Churchill was acutely aware that there was only a numerical superiority of seven dreadnoughts in the Royal Navy's favour, and to him these two ships represented a wonderful opportunity to increase the British strength. On the outbreak of war with Germany the Turkish vessels were requisitioned and commissioned as HMS *Agincourt* and *Erin*. Whatever Churchill's motives were for this action in either the short or long term – and after the signing of the German-Turkish treaty on the 2nd how easy it would have been for the Turkish crew to have sailed the *Sultan Osman* across the North Sea to a German port – it provoked a violent anti-British campaign in Turkey. To make matters worse the arrival of the *Goeben* and *Breslau* in Constantinople was seen by many Turks as indicative of their true friends.★

Within days of the arrival of the two ships in Constantinople Rear Admiral Arthur Limpus, who had headed the British Naval Mission so successfully, was withdrawn from access to the Fleet and later was asked to leave the country altogether. Souchon's officers replaced the British and Souchon himself became Commander-in-Chief of the Turkish Navy, reflecting the growing German influence in Constantinople in the wake of the now discredited British. But, until Turkey's official attitude really became known, it was important to do nothing to drive her further into the German camp.

With the *Goeben* and *Breslau* in Turkish waters the general direction of operations in the Mediterranean was to be in the hands of the French, while many of the British ships were withdrawn for service

---

★ Two other battleships building for Chile were also taken over during the war with far less serious consequences. One of them was to have been named the *Almirante Cochrane*, commemorating Lord Cochrane's service to Chile. This ship was subsequently converted to become the aircraft carrier HMS *Eagle*.

elsewhere. Sir Berkeley Milne, being senior to the French Commander-in-Chief, Vice-Admiral Augustin Boué de Lapeyrère, was ordered
to return home. Rear Admiral Sackville Carden, promoted Vice-
Admiral at the end of August, who was the Admiral Superintendent at
Malta, thus by a quirk of fate became the Senior British Naval Officer
in the Mediterranean. Rear Admiral Troubridge, who was shortly to
take the blame for the escape of the two German ships even though he
was cleared later by a court-martial, was left temporarily in command
of the British ships watching the Dardanelles in case the two German
ships – or were they then Turkish? – should leave.

At the age of 57 Rear Admiral Carden would in the normal way
have expected to retire at the end of an undemanding appointment in
Malta. But war was now to change that. Although he had seen active
service during his career it can hardly be thought that either action in
the Egyptian and Sudan campaigns of 1882–84 or in the Benin Gulf
expedition of 1897 would prepare him for the coming months in the
Eastern Mediterranean. But there were no serving senior officers who
had the experience of commanding a fleet in action. Promoted in 1908
to Rear Admiral, he had only hoisted his flag at sea for one year in
HMS *London* in the Atlantic Fleet, when he was second-in-command
to Vice-Admiral John Jellicoe.

On 10 September Admiral Troubridge sailed for England to attend
the Court of Inquiry investigating the escape of the *Goeben* and
Breslau. In his place Churchill had wished to appoint Admiral Limpus
who had finally left Turkey on the 16th. Regrettably the Foreign
Office, who were still desperately trying to ensure that the Turks
remained neutral, persuaded the Prime Minister that such an appointment would be 'unduly provocative' and Carden was ordered to take
command of the ships watching the Dardanelles while Limpus, a
much more able officer, went to Malta. It was a useless gesture for
Turkey entered the war on the side of Germany on 5 November.
Strangely, even then neither Churchill nor Fisher, who at that time
came back as First Sea Lord, took action to put the right man in the
right job, and Carden remained for several more crucial months.
Indeed, it seems that despite his vast practical knowledge and
experience of the Turks and Turkey Limpus was ignored and his
advice spurned throughout the coming campaign. It was one more
blunder among all too many.

The pursuing British ships remained off the entrance to the

Dardanelles waiting in case the *Goeben* and *Breslau* showed themselves, and with instructions to sink them whether they flew the German or the Turkish ensign.

From Admiralty
   To Vice-Admiral Carden, Malta.   21 September

Assume command of the squadron off the Dardanelles. Your sole duty is to sink the *Goeben* and *Breslau*, no matter what flag they fly, if they come out of the Dardanelles. We are not at war with Turkey but German Admiral Souchon is now C.-in-C. Turkish Navy and Germans are controlling and largely manning it. Turks have been told that any Turkish ships which come out with *Goeben* and *Breslau* will equally be attacked by us. You are authorised to act accordingly without further declaration or parley.

In Constantinople Souchon worked hard to consolidate the new German popularity and his own position in the Turkish Navy, while striving to ensure that the out-dated Turkish fleet was brought to a state of readiness for war. It was the end of October before he felt ready to make his next move – a series of co-ordinated attacks on the Russian fleet in their Black Sea ports including the bases of Sevastopol and Odessa. The result was predictable. On the 30th the Russian, British and French Ambassadors protested strongly to the Turks and then asked for their passports to return home. The Turks were given twelve hours to send home all the Germans from the crews of the two ships, including Souchon, and to demobilize. Russia declared war on 2 November. The following day British ships shelled the forts at the entrance to the Dardanelles to emphasize their determination and to influence the Turks to accede to their demands. It did no such thing, and Britain and France declared war on the 5th.

With that one bombardment completed the Allied ships off the Dardanelles resumed their watch for any move by the two ex-German ships. Yet both Fisher and Churchill were eager for the Royal Navy to be seen to be active; both had their eyes firmly fixed on impossible schemes for the Baltic. As early in the war as 19 August Churchill had written to the Russian Commander-in-Chief, the Grand Duke Nicholas, proposing a joint operation in which Russian troops would be landed on the Pomeranian coast of North Germany under cover of the guns of the British fleet. Later, in October, at a meeting of

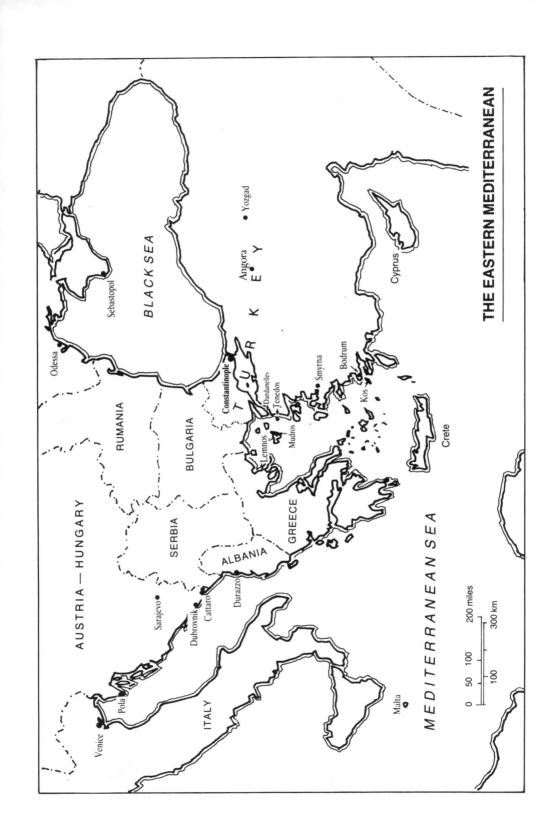

THE EASTERN MEDITERRANEAN

AUSTRIA — HUNGARY

BLACK SEA

Sebastopol

Odessa

RUMANIA

BULGARIA

SERBIA

Sarajevo

Dubrovnik
Cattaro

Durazzo

ALBANIA

Constantinople

T · U · R
K
E · Y

Angora

Yozgad

GREECE

Dardanelles
Tenedos

Smyrna

Bodrum

Kos

Lemnos

Mudros

Cyprus

Crete

Pola

Venice

ITALY

Malta

MEDITERRANEAN SEA

0   50   100   200 miles

100   300 km

Admirals of the Grand Fleet there was much discussion about a possible attack on Heligoland or Borkum as a preliminary to sending ships to the Baltic.

Fisher always maintained that the best place for the British army was on the flanks or in amphibious operations where it could be supported by the Navy. Yet throughout the war the majority of the British Army remained virtually static in trenches in Northern France, as part of the left wing of the massive French army but with French and Belgian divisions between it and the sea. It came to man the line southward from the famous Ypres Salient by chance in the early battles of 1914, and, perhaps for political reasons as much as by military necessity, there it remained with only minor adjustments for the next four years.

The idea of an attack on the Dardanelles was first discussed at a meeting of the War Council on 25 November as a means of relieving Turkish pressure on Egypt. The idea was put forward by Fisher, with the support of Churchill, that a joint attack would put pressure on the Turks forcing them to withdraw troops threatening the Suez Canal. If, by such an attack, the Turks could also be put out of the war it would then reopen the supply route to Russia which was so desperately short of war supplies and whose economy was tottering as men from the factories were conscripted in large numbers into the army which had neither the weapons to arm them nor the means of training them adequately. The proposal came to nought since Kitchener had no troops to spare for such a venture and neither he nor the French would countenance any reduction in the number of troops already in France.

Such a problem had been considered by the General Staff in 1906 and studied by the Committee for Imperial Defence the following year. On neither occasion was such a plan considered to be feasible without undue risk and large numbers of troops. Yet there was a precedent. In 1807 Vice-Admiral Sir John Duckworth with seven ships of the line, two frigates and two bomb ships passed up the Dardanelles into the Sea of Marmara to threaten Constantinople. He reached his objective with minimal casualties and then, after ten days during which he failed to bring the Turkish fleet to action or to threaten the capital, he used a shift in the wind to return to the Aegean. His casualties for this second passage of the Straits were considerably heavier. The episode proves little when considering whether or not the Dardanelles could be forced by ships alone, for undoubtedly a Nelson – or even Lord Cochrane – would have ensured a different ending. Nevertheless it should have provided a warning as to what could ensue if the Fleet arrived in the Marmara without a clear objective, or if the Turks proved more resilient than expected with their capital under fire.

In September the three B-class submarines from Malta, the *B9*, *B10* and *B11*, had arrived to join the blockading force with their equally elderly depot ship, the converted merchant ship *Hindu Kush*. There they were joined by a number of French submarines, the *Brumaire* and *Circe* being the first to arrive. The latter dated from 1907 while the *Brumaire* was slightly larger and more modern, yet neither could be said to be any more effective than smaller, obsolescent British boats.

Emphasizing the lack of a secure base for the force off the Dardanelles was the fact that the repair ship *HMS Blenheim*, the *Hindu Kush*, the destroyers and the submarines were based on the anchorage on the south side of the island of Tenedos, the whole force having to move to the north side whenever the wind changed. The French submarines with their external torpedoes were particularly susceptible to the weather and found the conditions in the open anchorages very trying. Tenedos, a small island only a short distance to the south of the entrance to the Dardanelles, was at that time technically Greek, and therefore neutral, having been captured from the Turks in 1912, but along with other nearby islands it was to play an increasingly important part in keeping the British and French ships in the area supplied.

It was recognized that it was impossible for any of the submarines present to penetrate all the way up the Dardanelles into the Sea of Marmara – their endurance was too limited – but it was thought that one might be able to get as far as Chanak, attack any shipping that might be found and still return safely. The *B11*, commanded by Lieutenant Norman Holbrook RN, was the only one of the allied submarines to have been recently refitted with a new, and hence fairly reliable, battery. Nevertheless she was old and out-dated but it was considered that she had a fair chance of success and in any case an operation of this sort would break the monotony of the short and profitless patrols across the entrance to the Straits.

Before sailing, the staff of the *Blenheim* fitted the submarine with guards to protect the hydroplanes and prevent them fouling the mooring wires of any mines that might be met. Then, early on the morning of 13 December she got under way, an inauspicious date for such a great adventure. And so it must have seemed, for almost immediately she was forced to stop when one of the new hydroplane guards fouled her own mooring wires; the trouble was cleared within minutes. Creeping up to within a mile of Cape Helles at the southern end of the Gallipoli peninsula Holbrook dived to begin his perilous passage, making good a steady two knots and keeping close in to the European shore. With Cape Helles abeam he went to 60 feet to avoid any mines, only coming back to periscope depth every so often to check his position, showing only the smallest amount of periscope, lest it, or the feather wake from it, be seen by some alert sentry. After over four hours when his periscope broke surface he saw over towards the Asiatic shore the old battleship *Messudieh* lying at anchor. Holbrook ordered a turn to starboard across the current to close the range and bring his two torpedo tubes to bear. Before firing he increased speed to full to help his First Lieutenant, Sidney Winn, keep the boat in trim for to show themselves at this stage would have almost certainly ruined their chances of a successful attack. Fifteen minutes after sighting his target he fired his starboard torpedo and then was caught by the fierce current swinging him violently off course and preventing him firing his second torpedo. The Turks caught sight of the *B11*'s periscope as Winn tried unsuccessfully to control the submarine and opened fire. The *B11* then grounded on a shoal leaving her with conning tower exposed and under the fire of the now thoroughly alerted Turkish batteries, but though straddled she managed to slide off into deeper water without being hit. The *Messudieh* was hit aft, capsized and sank in about ten minutes. Holbrook now had the problem of returning down the Straits with the Turks keenly looking for any sign of him and the submarine's battery rapidly becoming exhausted. The air was tainted with petrol fumes, making breathing difficult, while the helmsman was having problems reading the compass as the lens was fogged. Several times taken off course by eddies but aided by the current, Holbrook managed to get his boat and the weary crew clear of Cape Helles once again, surfacing just after 2.0 pm, having been dived for nearly nine hours. Oh! The wonderful taste of fresh air! The crew quickly recovered, although it took longer for the air to become fresh enough to start the petrol engine.

Nine days later Holbrook was awarded the first naval Victoria Cross of the war, Sidney Winn receiving the DSO and the whole crew received DSMs.

Regretfully the pleasure of the submariners at Holbrook's success in sinking the Turkish ship and his award of the VC was dampened the following month. The French submarine *Saphir* tried to repeat Holbrook's achievement. Exactly what happened is not known, but they reached as far as the Narrows and then ran aground off Nagara Point and were lost.

On 22 November the Turkish army launched an offensive against newly-won Russian positions in the Caucasus. It later became known as the Battle of Sarikamish. The intensity of the fighting may be gauged from the fact that before it was over both sides had lost nearly 100,000 men killed, though the weather may have claimed almost as many victims as the enemy. The battle lasted until mid-January and ended in an overwhelming defeat for the Turks. Little known now outside a small circle of military historians and fought in a remote area, the battle was to have repercussions out of all proportion to its own importance for it became the immediate cause of the most controversial campaign of the war, which in its turn was to cost Britain, the Empire and her Allies dearly.

By the end of December the Russian army was falling back before the offensive and the British Cabinet received on 2 January, 1915, an appeal from the Russian Commander-in-Chief for some form of action that would ease the pressure in the Caucasus. When this appeal was originally sent through the British Ambassador in Petrograd the Russian predicament was very real yet within days the situation was to change dramatically and it was the Turkish army that was in retreat. But by then the British had sent a reply indicating that some action would be initiated against the Turks. But what action, and where?

Inevitably, the Dardanelles came to be considered as the only possible area in which we could help. Fisher immediately drew up a memorandum for Churchill's consideration and which could be given to the Cabinet. His plan was in two parts, requiring both naval and military participation. On the military side he proposed a combined attack with regular British troops, which would have to be withdrawn from France, on the Gallipoli Peninsula with Greek participation. At the same time the Bulgars would open an offensive directly towards Constantinople. The Navy would simultaneously attack up the

Dardanelles using some of the many pre-Dreadnought battleships which were still in commission and whose loss would not affect the precarious balance of power between the fleets in the North Sea. He concluded, in typical Fisher manner with the words in capital letters, stressing the need for urgent action for without it FAILURE!

His idea was doomed from the start. Neither Kitchener nor the French would allow the withdrawal of any troops from the Western Front, which was regarded as of prime importance, and where they considered there were not enough troops anyway. Then again, while the Greeks and the Bulgars both hated the Turks, they were hardly more friendly to each other and both had sizeable pro-German factions in their Governments. In any case both countries were still neutral and would have to be persuaded to declare war before such a plan could be considered.

Nevertheless Churchill seized upon the last part of the plan and, despite Fisher's statement that any naval attempt on the Dardanelles was only a part of the whole, he decided that this was the only way to help the Russians. It would also be the opportunity for the Navy to be actively engaged, something for which he continually pressed. Indeed, that afternoon he signalled to Carden asking whether he considered that the Dardanelles could be forced 'by the use of ships alone'.

Carden's reply indicated that he did not think that the Dardanelles could be rushed, but that they might be forced in stages in extended operations by a large number of ships. This was what Churchill wanted to hear and Carden was ordered to prepare a more detailed operational plan. Despite Churchill's enthusiasm and Carden's cautious agreement, such an operation had not been Fisher's intention at all, and overlooked the basic fact that naval guns with their flat trajectories were unsuitable for the task, unlike the German heavy siege howitzers used so successfully at Liège and Antwerp. But nobody could, or would, stop Churchill. No one in the Cabinet called a halt, no one pointed out that the operation could be postponed until more forces could be made available for a properly planned and co-ordinated naval and military assault. This was a plan conceived in urgency to give support to the Russians, yet more than six weeks were to pass before any action began. In that time the Russian army in the Caucasus had survived the crisis on their own, and in their turn had beaten the Turks. Properly planned and with sufficient forces this was just the role which Fisher foresaw for the Army and Navy working together; it just might have succeeded. But the history of war can easily be re-written with the benefit of hindsight and the use of the word "if".

Admiral Carden began his attack on the morning of Friday 19 February, with the ships opening fire at long range but during the afternoon closing in to 6,000 yards (3 nautical miles). They then withdrew, while overnight the weather intervened, a storm causing a halt to any further operations until the 25th. Once again the forts were pounded at close range after which sailors and marines were sent ashore to complete the destruction of the emplacements after they had been abandoned by the enemy. As the battleships advanced further into the Straits they were preceded by minesweepers, mostly converted trawlers and still manned by their civilian crews. It seemed that Churchill might have been right to choose this course and Carden's signal on 2 March that he hoped to be off Constantinople in fourteen days was received with great delight.

Yet, six days later the minesweepers had been halted by the fire of the Turkish guns and the battleships could not go forward without the minesweepers to clear the mines. Naval crews were put into the sweepers and though some progress was made the cost in minesweepers was high. It began to look like a stalemate.

Urged on from London by Churchill and thwarted by ever stiffer Turkish resistance Carden's health gave way and the medical advice was that he should return home. Here was another chance to make use of Admiral Limpus' experience, but he remained in Malta while Carden's second-in-command, Rear Admiral John de Robeck took command of the allied force.

Roger Keyes, who had been so rapidly relieved of his appointment as Commodore at Harwich, had arrived in Malta on 14 February to become the Chief of Staff to Admiral Carden. He had been with Carden when the opening shots of the campaign were fired. It was Keyes who had been responsible for putting volunteer naval crews in the minesweepers to stiffen their resolve and had instituted sweeping by night to try and reduce the damage to the ships from gunfire. Now he was to stay as Chief of Staff to de Robeck.

De Robeck was 52 years of age when he was given this command. Irish born, he had entered the Navy in 1875 but in the intervening years had seen no active service. He had been promoted Rear Admiral in 1911 and the following year had been given the new appointment as Admiral of Patrols, responsible for the defence of the coasts of the United Kingdom. On the outbreak of war he had been without an appointment but had been given the 9th Cruiser Squadron, commissioning from reserve. With the decision to try and force the Dardanelles, he had been sent as second-in-command to Carden, and the two men had worked together in the planning of the operation that he was now so suddenly to command.

There occurred one other incident at about this time which was to play an important part in future events. Until early March the Allied ships had had no secure base for their operations closer than Alexandria in Egypt or Malta. Then on the 7th the island of Lemnos was occupied by troops sent from Egypt. The island, like Tenedos, had been captured by the Greeks during the Balkan Wars and now with the connivance of the pro-British Greek Prime Minister, M. Venizelos, the Greek garrison was withdrawn. Even the defences were left undisturbed for the British to occupy, the island being technically Turkish again with the withdrawal of the Greeks. At this stage Venizelos offered Greek troops and their fleet for the attack on Gallipoli, but this led to his resignation when the King refused to support his war-like policy, and he was replaced by the less friendly M. Gounaris. Still the occupation of the island went ahead and Rear Admiral Rosslyn Wemyss was selected as Military Governor. In the months to come it was to be Wemyss who would take charge of this valuable base built up around the great natural harbour of Mudros.

With a new Commander the fleets prepared to renew the attack with every confidence of success. March 18 dawned a fine spring day and the first wave of British battleships led by the new *Queen Elizabeth* with her 15-inch guns opened a heavy fire on the forts. Then the French battleships joined in. As the third line was ordered up the second ship in the French line, the *Bouvet*, took a hit which penetrated the magazine. She blew up and sank within two minutes with the loss of over 600 men. Despite this loss the bombardment continued but under intensified return fire from the shore as if the Turkish gunners had been heartened by this success. Then the battle-cruiser *Inflexible* hit a mine and she had to limp away, eventually going to Malta for extensive repairs in the dockyard. Then the old battleship *Irresistible* hit another mine. The *Ocean* and the *Swiftsure* went to the aid of their disabled comrade but were unable to take her in tow and two hours later the *Ocean*, which had continued firing at the enemy forts from her position near the *Irresistible*, was also mined. Both the *Ocean* and the *Irresistible* sank later while the *Agamemnon* and the French *Gaulois* had been hit by the end of the day when the action was called off. With darkness the ships sailed away to regroup and repair the damage.

It had not been a good day for de Robeck, with three of his ships sunk, two crippled and another damaged, besides the damage to a number of the minesweepers. Yet the Turks were in a bad way themselves; they had few mines left and were forced to use Russian ones which were carefully recovered from the Bosphorus. The forts had used over half their ammunition and had little armour-piercing shell left. A Turkish account reveals that Fort Hamidieh on the Asiatic shore had but five or ten rounds left, and that even the German gunners were convinced that they could not go on much longer and that the fleet must get through. In Constantinople there was a general expectation that the Allied ships would appear at any time and a feeling of panic spread throughout the city. How tempting to speculate on what might have been!

The following day a gale prevented a resumption of the bombardment, but when the weather cleared the fleet did not return to the attack. Keyes alone was anxious to make another attempt and give the enemy no chance to rebuild their defences. Neither de Robeck nor Wemyss agreed with him, believing that in this case his ever-adventurous spirit was not the answer to the problem.

Major-General Birdwood, who commanded the Australian and New Zealand troops in Egypt, had joined the naval force as an observer. On the day following the disastrous naval attack he signalled his views to Kitchener:

> The Straits are not likely to be forced by battleships, as at one time seemed probable, and that if my troops took part, it will not take the subsidiary form anticipated. The army's part will be more than mere landing parties to destroy the forts: it must be a deliberate and prepared military operation carried out at full strength so as to open the passage for the Navy.

It was to be the task of the army to land on the Gallipoli Peninsula. Kitchener had already agreed that the 29th Infantry Division could be made available instead of being sent to France, and this, with the Royal

Naval Division, a French division plus two divisions of Australians and New Zealanders would give a force of over 75,000 men. The only problems were how soon and how efficiently they could be made ready to attack an enemy that would surely know that this was the only alternative and that a landing would be made.

Table II: Characteristics of Dardanelles Submarines

	HMS B11	HMS E7	GERMAN U21	GERMAN UB 8	FRENCH Saphir (2)	FRENCH Joule (3)
Completed	1906	1914	1913	1915	1908	1902
Length	142 ft 2½ ins	178 ft 1 ins	211 ft 10¼ ins	92 ft 9 ins	147 ft 4 ins	170 ft 11 ins
Beam	13 ft 7 ins	22 ft 8½ ins	20 ft 1½ ins	10 ft 7 ins	12 ft 10 ins	17 ft 9 ins
Surface Displacement	287 tons	655 tons	650 tons	127 tons	392 tons	397 tons
Dived Displacement	316 tons	796 tons	837 tons	142 tons	425 tons	551 tons
Torpedo Tubes	2 × 18 ins	4 × 18 ins (1)	4 × 50 cm	2 × 45 cm	6 × 45 cm	1 × 45 cm plus 6 torpedoes external
Surface Speed	12 knots	15.25 knots	15.4 knots	6.5 knots	11.5 knots	13 knots
Dived Speed	6.5 knots	9.0 knots	9.5 knots	5.5 knots	9.2 knots	8.8 knots
Surface Endurance	1300 miles at 9.0 knots	3000 miles at 10.0 knots	7600 miles at 8 knots	1650 miles at 5 knots	2000 miles at 7.3 knots	1700 miles at 10 knots
Dived Endurance	50 miles at 4.5 knots	99 miles at 3 knots	80 miles at 5 knots	45 miles at 4 knots	100 miles at 5 knots	84 miles at 5 knots
Crew	15	30	35	14	21	29

(1) *E11* and higher numbered boats similar but with extra bow tube. (2) *Turquoise* similar. (3) *Bernouilli* similar.

9

The Dardanelles –
The Submarines Gather

IT HAS BEEN recorded that early arrivals to join the Allied fleet off the Dardanelles were the British B-class submarines from Malta, supported by the *Hindu Kush* together with a number of French boats. In the months that followed the *B11* gained everlasting fame with Holbrook while the *Saphir* was lost in early 1915. It was obvious that none of these elderly submarines could hope to reach the Sea of Marmara and that nothing more could be done in this respect until some of the new E-class could be spared from duty in the North Sea.

The first to arrive was the Australian HMAS *AE2* under the command of Lieutenant-Commander H. G. Stoker RN and manned with a crew half each of British and Australian ratings, but she came not from the North Sea but from the Pacific. The *AE2*, with her sister *AE1*, had arrived in Sydney not long before the war, the first submarines of the infant Royal Australian Navy. The latter was unfortunately accidentally lost in circumstances which are still unknown near Rabaul in the Bismarck Archipelago in the first few days of the war. When the danger to Australia from the German Asiatic Squadron was over, after the Battle of the Falkland Islands in December, 1914, Stoker was ordered to return to the Mediterranean with his submarine. They joined the fleet off Tenedos in February, having passed through the Suez Canal to the cheers of the troops on guard there and waiting for the expected Turkish attack which could have come at any time.

At the beginning of 1915 the main worry for the British and French commanders over enemy submarines centred on the Austrian boats based in the Adriatic, as they had only a comparatively short distance to travel to reach the fleet off the Dardanelles. But on the very day that Carden's ships began their bombardment of the forts the Admiralty sent a warning that German submarines might try and pass through the Straits of Gibraltar. Much bigger and newer than the Austrian boats, their presence in the Eastern Mediterranean would present a considerable threat to Carden's plans.

To reach the Mediterranean would be a long passage for any submarine coming from Germany and the most dangerous part would undoubtedly be the Straits of Gibraltar. On patrol in that area was a light cruiser, a destroyer and a number of elderly torpedo boats. However, their chances of detecting a determined submarine were small since the submarine could pass through the area covered by the patrols without having to surface, and these ships had no method of detecting a dived submarine. Until the middle of February the three old submarines HMS *B6, B7* and *B8* had also been based on Gibraltar and had been used to supplement these anti-submarine patrols. Then it was decided that they would be of greater use at the other end of the Mediterranean; the *B6* and the *B8* arrived at Mudros on 21st and the third boat shortly afterwards.

At this time Admiral Souchon felt that the Turkish navy would be strengthened by the addition of some submarines and sent a message to the Austrian Commander-in-Chief, Admiral Anton Haus, for some to be sent. The Austrians, however, had started the war with only six submarines which were comparable with the obsolescent British B and C classes, and since then they had received only two more; one of these was a privately built experimental vessel which was requisitioned and the other was the captured French *Curie*. Five other larger boats which had been building for the Austrian navy at Kiel were sold to the Germans, becoming the *U66–70*, as it was not considered practical for them to attempt the passage to Pola. In view of later events this was perhaps an overhasty decision and one that the Austrian navy regretted. It is not surprising therefore that when they were asked to send some of their small flotilla to Turkey they refused. Admiral Haus said that they had insufficient range and in any case were required in the Adriatic to defend the Austrian bases at Pola and Cattaro. With that unsatisfactory reply Souchon sent another request to Berlin that U-boats be sent to the Mediterranean, a request that was fully supported both by the Turkish Government and the German Ambassador in Constantinople.

There were two ways that the Germans could help. The most obvious involved sending one or more of the newer larger U-boats from Germany through the Straits of Gibraltar, a move that the Admiralty in London had anticipated. Alternatively a number of the new small UB or UC type submarines could be taken in sections to Pola where they could be re-assembled and then complete their journey to Turkey through the Mediterranean. This latter course was the one that was initially adopted, and six boats were earmarked for shipment.

In October, 1914, designs had been put forward for two new classes of small U-boat which could be built in quick time. As a result seventeen coastal submarines, known as the UB type, with ten small minelayers of the UC type were initially ordered. The UB boats, known by their crews as 'tin tadpoles', had a surface displacement of only 127 tons and a length of under 100 feet. The original design featured only an electric motor with all the inherent limitations involved, an idea which had been discarded over a decade previously. However, sanity prevailed and one 60hp diesel engine was added to the design and gave a surface speed of about 6½ knots. The armament was two 45cm torpedoes, no reloads being carried within the tiny hull. The UC boats were only slightly larger, carrying their mines in twelve external mine chutes, but because of their small size it was not possible to include any torpedo armament in the design.

Each of these submarines consisted of three main sections and for the journey to Pola these sections were loaded on to railway waggons. Other waggons carried the conning tower, engines, batteries and parts of the casing. At Pola the waggons were unloaded and the submarine re-assembled, a task which was estimated to take about fourteen working days. Plans to send the *UB16* and *UB17* direct to Constantinople for assembly in the Stenia Yard proved to be impracticable. The first boat to leave Germany was the *UB8* which arrived in Pola on 26 March, 1915, and the task of re-assembling the sections was started at once. It was a remarkable feat for in just over a month Leutnant von Voigt had the sea trials completed and was able to take his tiny craft off on her voyage to Turkey.

Having completed with stores and fuel at Porto Palazzo on Meleda Island (off the coast north of Dubrovnik and now known as Mljet) von

Voigt sailed in tow of the Austrian cruiser *Novara* on 4 May, the cruiser helping the small submarine on her way not only for protection but also to save fuel. At about 3 o'clock that afternoon with the submarine towing at 9½ knots the bow suddenly dipped. The Navigating Officer, who was on watch on the bridge, was unable to slip the tow and was only able to throw the conning tower hatch shut at the last moment before the whole submarine went under. The *UB8* went quickly down to 60 feet with water pouring in through the unclipped hatch while the three men who had been on the bridge were left swimming for their lives. The *Novara* stopped at once which brought the submarine back to the surface like a yo-yo. One man was drowned and von Voigt had to return to harbour with the *UB8* to repair the damage and clean up the mess inside the boat. He was able to sail again the next day!

The troubles of the *UB8* were not over. Three days later the wind strengthened quickly to force 8. The small submarine rolled so badly that von Voigt feared that the battery acid would be split and he was forced to heave to. The motion then changed to a fierce energy-sapping pitching with seas washing over the conning tower. Fearing further damage, particularly to his hydroplanes, von Voigt took the boat down to 60 feet to ride out the storm, though even there the motion was quite noticeable and unpleasant for those with weak stomachs. Eventually he reached Orak, near Bodrum on the Gulf of Kos, on 11 May where he found supplies of fuel and provisions had been arranged for him. On the 13th the submarine set off again to begin operations against the fleet off the Dardanelles, but her gyro compass broke down and, with an unreliable magnetic compass, von Voigt put into Smyrna for repairs. The sixteen day passage had been very strenous for the small boat; the limited accommodation gave little respite for the off-watch crew while the weather and the long time they had been forced to spend submerged had taxed both machinery and battery to the limit.

The next boat to be sent was the *UB7* under the command of Leutnant Werner. Having left Pola on 11 May she arrived safely at Orak on the 20th. A third boat, the *UB3*, reported herself some 80 miles from Smyrna on 23 May but was not heard of again.

The Germans had also considered sending a U-boat from Germany to the Mediterranean. Otto Hersing, the commander of the *U21*, was selected for the task. He had already made a name for himself when he had penetrated the Firth of Forth to sink HMS *Pathfinder* and since then had been successful in the Bay of Seine where he had intercepted and sunk two merchant ships after their crews had been ordered to abandon ship. If any officer could reach the Mediterranean then it was felt that Hersing could. On 18 March Admiral Souchon was told that the *U21* would leave for the Mediterranean at the beginning of April, yet it was the 25th before everything was ready and Hersing sailed from Wilhelmshaven. Eluding allied patrols and deliberately abstaining from attacks on shipping, he chose the long route around the north of Scotland and effected a rendezvous off Cape Finisterre a week later with the steamer *Marzala*.

After a quick exchange of recognition signals the submarine followed the merchantman into the Rio de Corcubin on the west coast of Spain and, while the steamer anchored, Hersing brought his boat alongside. Quickly the two crews got to work and the night was spent embarking stores, lubricating oil and another 12½ tons of fuel to supplement the 56 tons which had been on board when he had left Germany. The following day at sea it was found that the new fuel was the wrong sort and quite useless for the *U21's* engines. Hersing had barely 26 tons of useable fuel on board and he was not yet half way to Cattaro. To go back meant a long delay while to go on would be fraught with difficulty. IF the remainder of the passage could be accomplished without too much time dived, IF he could proceed at economical speed while on the surface, about 9 knots, and IF the weather remained fair, then he decided that he would have a good chance of reaching his new base.

At dawn on 6 May Hersing was entering the Straits of Gibraltar close to the Moroccan coast. That afternoon he sighted two torpedo boats of the Straits patrol and was forced to dive, one of them opening fire briefly and ineffectively on his periscope. Two days later he had a meeting with a merchant ship which again forced him to dive. In misty weather a steamer was almost abeam of the submarine before both vessels sighted each other at what must have been almost the same moment. As the steamer altered towards so the submarine dived. When south of Sicily Hersing was sighted by two French destroyers which opened fire on his periscope and forced him to remain dived for some hours as they hunted for him in vain. The *U21* arrived at Cattaro on 13 May without further incident but with less than two tons of fuel remaining.

Since Stoker's arrival off Tenedos with the *AE2* in February he had been determined that the Australian submarine would be the first to make the passage up the 35 miles of the Dardanelles into the Sea of Marmara. Any submarine attempting to reach the Marmara would have to overcome a number of obstacles, not the least being a strong current which flowed continuously into the Mediterranean from the Black Sea. It was known that the Turks had laid mines and that the guns and the searchlights in the many forts would preclude any attempt to go through on the surface, even at night. Dived navigation would not be very easy since too much use of the periscope would be sure to lead to detection, yet, at the Narrows, just north of Chanak, the Straits were no wider than half a mile and dog-legged in shape. Following the opening bombardments by Carden's battleships, Stoker believed that an attempt to pass up the Straits could be made under cover of the attack, using the presence of the big ships to go as far as possible on the surface, and that the chance of success was good 'if one exercised the greatest possible care in navigation'.

The *AE2* was returning to Mudros with Stoker determined to put his plan to the Admiral when fate intervened. The night was dark – no moon and the sky starless, while heavy rain squalls blanketed all navigational marks. In the long swell brought on by the strong southerly wind they met the French destroyer guarding the entrance and flashed the recognition letters in answer to the challenge and then picked up the dim white light marking the entrance. What Stoker was not told was that the light on Sangrala Point in the middle of the harbour had been extinguished, and the submarine ran aground. Although the submarine bumped heavily in the swell on the rocks and it was morning before she could be towed off she was not too badly damaged and she was able to go to Malta under her own power for repairs. For an enterprise which, by Stoker's own words, demanded the greatest possible care in navigation it was not the best time to put his idea before the Admiral.

On 7 April Stoker was in Malta watching the Dockyard carry out the necessary repairs to the *AE2* and there was joined by the *E11, E14* and *E15* with their depot ship *HMS Adamant* which had been sailed from Harwich to join the fleet in the Eastern Mediterranean. Next morning the *Adamant* went on with the *E14* and *E15* leaving Nasmith and his boat behind to carry out repairs to the armature of the port motor and to the starboard intermediate shaft. Both Stoker and

Nasmith were keen to get their boats out of the Dockyard and ready for action. That Nasmith was the first away was only because he arranged for the new intermediate shaft to be sent direct to Mudros to be machined and fitted by the repair ship, rather than wait in the Dockyard. The *E11* arrived to join the *Adamant* and the other submarines on 18 April to be greeted with the sad news of the loss of the *E15*.

The *E15*, commanded by Lieutenant-Commander T. S. Brodie, who in the early days of the war had commanded the *D8* at Harwich, had sailed the day before Nasmith's arrival with the intention of breaking through the Dardanelles into the Sea of Marmara. Brodie intended to be off the European shore opposite Kephez Bay, not far short of Holbrook's earlier exploit, at daybreak, and would thus have the benefit of daylight for the tricky task of navigating through the Narrows. However, the boat had been caught in a strong eddy and swept on to a shoal near Kephez Point right under the guns of one of the forts. Although at first the boat was undamaged, Brodie was unable to work her off the shoal into the safety of deeper water. Then a shell exploded on the conning tower and killed Brodie as he was climbing out of the hatch, while a second shell killed three more ratings. The remainder of the crew took to the water from where they were picked up and made prisoners.

The news of this disaster was brought back by Commander C. R. Samson of the Royal Navy Air Service who had flown over the area and seen the *E15* lying apparently undamaged in shoal water. Flying with Samson was Lieutenant-Commander C. G. Brodie, twin brother of the unfortunate submarine commanding officer, and himself a submariner though at that time serving on de Robeck's staff with Keyes. The problem now facing the British was to prevent the Turks salving the *E15* and using her against them and to ensure that any secret equipment and papers still on board were destroyed. It was not known until after the war that, in fact, all the confidential papers and charts were burned by the surviving officers before they abandoned the boat.

First, the old submarine HMS *B6*, under the command of Lieutenant C. G. MacArthur, was sent into the Straits with instructions to torpedo the stranded submarine, but was unable to do so. Strangely, MacArthur fired only one torpedo at the *E15* when at a range of 1200 to 1300 yards. He then altered course 180° to shape course for the open sea, retiring from the scene without trouble. Although some stories state that this torpedo exploded and sank a lighter lying alongside the *E15* this is not so. The torpedo was later recovered, having failed to explode.

That night two destroyers, HMS *Scorpion* and *Grampus*, were detailed to try where the *B6* had failed, the former commanded by Lieutenant-Commander Andrew B. Cunningham, and again with Charles Brodie on board to give professional advice. The story is told that while waiting for darkness to start the operation Cunningham and Brodie were startled to hear a bumping sound alongside the destroyer. Racing on deck and fearing that a mine was about to blow them all sky high they were surprised to find that the cause of the trouble was a floating torpedo. It was the one fired by MacArthur that morning which had come down the Straits with the current. Luckily the torpedo was secured before it could do any damage, the firing pistol which was in an armed state was removed and the whole was returned to the submariners the next morning 'with the compliments of HMS *Scorpion*'. Neither destroyer was able to locate the wreck later that night and, after coming under intense fire, though they were not hit, they were forced to retire.

The *B11*, still commanded by the now famous Holbrook, was the next to try and destroy the *E15*. Luck was not with Holbrook that day for thick fog came down, reducing visibility to almost nothing, and he too was forced to retire without even seeing the wreck. Bombardment by a battleship was found to be too inaccurate and the bombs dropped by a seaplane missed their target but did briefly disrupt the salvage work. It was left to torpedoes fired from improvised mountings fitted to two picket boats from the battleships *Triumph* and *Majestic* to ensure that the *E15* would never sail again. There was one more task for the *B6*. MacArthur had to take the long-suffering Brodie up the Straits once again to survey the wreck of his brother's submarine. The *E15* was observed from only 100 yards away lying on her starboard side heeled over beyond the horizontal showing only the bottom and the saddle tanks. Brodie was able to report that she was beyond salvage. While there the *B6* almost suffered the same fate, being caught in a violent eddy and was driven ashore not far from the *E15*. She broke surface and immediately came under heavy fire but MacArthur used full power to bump along the bottom and into the safety of deeper water without being hit. MacArthur himself was subsequently awarded the DSC for his part in those operations.

There is one more tale to tell of the unfortunate *E15*. A month after her loss the *Scorpion* and another destroyer, the *Wolverine*, commanded by Roger Keyes' younger brother Adrian, were operating up the Straits at night when Keyes thought he had an enemy submarine in sight and altered course to ram. Suddenly he realized that he was heading at full speed straight for the shore and the *E15*, and only at the last minute was able to avoid becoming another monument on the beach near Kephez Point.

Following hard on the heels of Nasmith and his *E11*, Stoker brought the *AE2* back from Malta, and he was chosen to make the next attempt on the Dardanelles. They were well up the Straits approaching Kephez when it was found that the shaft working the forward hydroplanes was broken, and, unable to dive, the *AE2* was forced to make a hasty withdrawal. With repairs made and a check dive completed Stoker reported to the Admiral and was instructed to try again. He left in the early hours of 25 April.

It has already been related that on that day Hersing set out from Germany bound for the Mediterranean. It was also the day when, at dawn, the Allied armies eventually landed on the Gallipoli peninsula. Stoker also made it the day on which an Australian submarine became the first to reach the Sea of Marmara. At seventy feet in the minefields beyond Kephez, the mooring wires of the mines made eerie scraping noises as they brushed past the hull, while coming shallow to check the position of the submarine through the periscope brought other hazards. Bright sun and an oily calm sea made the periscope all too easily sighted and the Turkish gunners were not slow to open fire. Even so Stoker found that progress was faster than he would have believed. He even took the opportunity of firing one of his precious torpedoes at a vessel which he believed might be laying mines and claimed a hit. He narrowly avoided being rammed by a destroyer and briefly went aground under the guns of the fort guarding the Narrows by Chanak. That evening they were on the surface in the Marmara to the east of Nagara thankfully recharging their batteries while the crew swarmed up on to the bridge, as many as possible at a time, to breathe the clean night air. From there Stoker was able to send a signal to de Robeck announcing his success.

This signal was received in the flagship as de Robeck, with Keyes as his Chief of Staff, together with the senior army commanders, were reviewing the results of the day's fighting ashore. The landings had

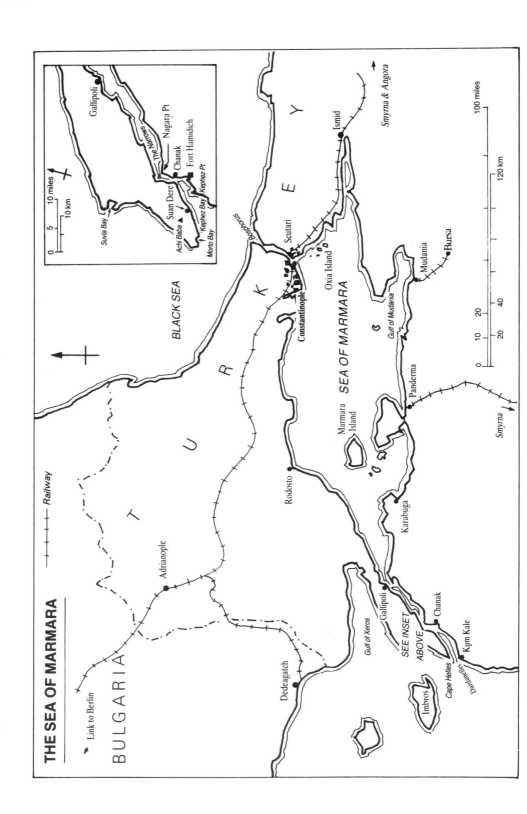

been fiercely opposed and casualties had been heavy, but at all except two places the troops with great gallantry had managed to establish their precarious bridgeheads. Even so, the generals were not sanguine about the future, and the possibility of re-embarkation was even discussed. At this stage Brodie again came on the scene, this time with Stoker's welcome message. The news that there was an Australian submarine in the Marmara threatening the Turkish lines of communication was very welcome indeed. For the next five days Stoker roamed the Sea of Marmara causing a certain amount of confusion but without specific success before having the satisfaction of a surprise meeting with the *E14*.

As soon as the news was received of Stoker's success in reaching the Marmara Keyes arranged for Lieutenant-Commander C. Boyle to join him with the *E14*. Boyle sailed in the early hours of 27 April and remained on the surface for as long as he could. At 4.0 am the searchlights by Suan Dere caught sight of the submarine and the guns immediately opened fire as Boyle dived to 90 feet to pass under the minefield.

> Rose to 22 feet [periscope depth] 1 mile south of Kilid Bahr [on the European shore opposite Chanak] and at 5.15 am passed Chanak, all the forts firing at me. There was a lot of small ships and steamboats patrolling and I saw one torpedo boat of the BERKI SATVET class [1014 tons] at which I fired one torpedo at a range of about 1600 yards. I just had time to see a large column of water as high as her mast rise from her quarter where she was presumably hit, when I had to go deep again. Some men in a small steam boat were leaning over trying to catch hold of the top of my periscope.

It sounds as if a lot of periscope was being shown for far too long a period of time. Nevertheless, Boyle got safely away and five hours later passed the town of Gallipoli at the neck of the peninsula and was able to alter course to the eastwards into the Sea of Marmara. Even so, there were several sailing ships, small steam boats and torpedo boats in sight and the *E14* remained dived until late afternoon when Boyle was able to give the order to surface and allow the crew to taste the fresh air again and to give the batteries some much-needed recharging.

Of the meeting between the *AE2* and the *E14* Boyle wrote in his report:

At 5.0 pm sighted AE2 and spoke to her. Stoker told me that they had had bad luck with their torpedoes, had sunk one gunboat and had one torpedo left. Arranged to meet the next day.

Yet indirectly this happy meeting of two strangers in an alien sea was to be the cause of the *AE2's* loss. Stoker had intended to be elsewhere the next day, but altered his plans to keep the arranged rendezvous with Boyle.

Early on 30 April the Turkish torpedo boat *Sultan Hissar* was returning to Constantinople when she sighted a submarine on the surface. As the torpedo boat altered course to close so the submarine dived. But something went wrong with the submarine's trim and she alternately went deep and broke surface, taking on large bow up or down angles in the process. With the *Sultan Hissar* firing rapidly and accurately with her small gun it was not long before she began to score vital hits. With water pouring in through holes in the hull the *AE2* surfaced for just long enough for all her crew to swim clear before she slid for the last time to the bottom of the Sea of Marmara.

Among the survivors of the *AE2* who were picked up by the *Sultan Hissar* was Able Seaman Albert Knaggs who had left the Royal Navy to join the Royal Australian Navy in 1913 while the *AE2* was still building. His diary of the events that followed survived the war, though unhappily Knaggs himself died in the POW camp at Kulu Maghara in October, 1916.

Then the torpedo boat lowered a boat to take us off in which there was a German officer, but she could only take five hands so we had to swim for it. When we got aboard we saw that her torpedo tubes were empty and a German sailor who could speak English told us they had both been fired at us but missed. Aboard the torpedo boat the officers were kept in the dark cabin while we were in the forward mess deck. While our clothes were being dried on deck the torpedo boat proceeded to Gallipoli and made fast alongside a hospital ship, where we were interviewed by General Liman von Sanders who was in command of the Peninsula. At 8.0 pm the torpedo boat proceeded to Constantinople where we arrived next morning. Before leaving the ship we were supplied with soldier suits, overcoats, slippers and red fezes to march through the streets of Constantinople to prison. The officers rode in a carriage.

On the same day that the *AE2* was lost the French submarine *Bernoulli* was sailed to attack Turkish shipping in the Straits below the

Narrows. The *Bernoulli* was one of a class of submarine only some ten feet shorter than the British E-class and a surface displacement about 250 tons lighter. In common with other French submarines the majority of the torpedoes were carried external to the hull. This time the *Bernoulli* found the current too much to cope with and was forced to return to the Aegean without having any success, or indeed having been sighted by the Turks. The following day her sister submarine, the *Joule*, left to join Boyle in the Marmara. Within hours the *Joule* and all her crew had been lost, blown up on one of the mines off Kephez. All that was left was part of one of her torpedoes which floated down on the current to be picked up by a patrolling destroyer.

Meanwhile Boyle continued to dominate the Sea of Marmara on his own. For three weeks his presence was reported to the Turkish authorities from all points of the compass. Of his eight torpedoes one was defective and could not be used, two missed their targets and one failed to explode despite hitting. Of the other four, all hit and Boyle claimed to have sunk two gunboats and two transports, the latter being used to hurry urgently needed re-inforcements to the army on the Gallipoli peninsula. On the debit side Boyle had had one periscope damaged by gunfire from a Turkish gunboat. His return on 18 May was comparatively uneventful though Boyle found it particularly galling to have to pass close to the Turkish battleship *Turgut Reiss* unable to attack as he had only a defective torpedo on board. The *E14* was cheered loudly as she passed through the fleet at the end of a momentous patrol. Boyle's report concludes simply with the words 'a small gun would have been invaluable'. How true!

The Admiralty for their part acted with commendable promptness when given the full story of this remarkable achievement. The award of the VC for Boyle was gazetted the following day while his officers were both given the DSC and all the crew the DSM.

Boyle had been given the word to return when Nasmith was finally able to report that the *E11* was fully repaired. The new intermediate shaft had arrived on board the *Reliance* from England and been machined to size, the pressure hull of the submarine had been opened up and the old shaft taken out and the new one fitted. The hull had then been securely riveted up again and tested for watertightness. As part of his preparations Nasmith had flown over the Straits in a two-seater Farman seaplane. Then, in the early hours of 19 May, after prayers on the casing around the conning tower, the *E11* set off from Mudros.

Nasmith kept the *E11* on the surface until the conical-shaped peak of Achi Baba – an isolated peak five miles north-east of Cape Helles which dominated the area and which was the scene of much bitter fighting – was abeam. His initial progress through the minefield to Kephez was quicker than he had expected and compared to both the *AE2* and *E14* he had a relatively easy passage. However, the submarine had been sighted and the two old battleships in the Straits which kept up a desultory bombardment on the British trenches hurriedly left the area for greater safety elsewhere and denied Nasmith the chance of a spectacular opening of his patrol. The *E11* was off the town of Gallipoli by 9.30 am and in the afternoon Nasmith took the submarine to rest on the bottom of the Sea of Marmara to wait for darkness and the chance to surface to charge the batteries and to renew the fetid air inside the submarine which by then made breathing difficult.

The fact that the submarines had had to go deep to avoid the minefields had opened the way for them to reach the Marmara successfully against the current, for at depths the current was reduced and then even reversed. One interesting old story was told to Nasmith of the days of one of the Sultans when an unwanted member of the household was dropped into the water from the walls of the Seraglio in an insufficiently weighted sack. Later, instead of being well away to the open sea it reappeared again – returned by the same current which years later was to help the submariners.

With Nasmith safely in the Sea of Marmara ready to begin operations, it is appropriate to continue the story of the German U-boats which were gathering in the Eastern Mediterranean, and of the Allied forces sent to seek them out. One patrol was established in the vicinity of the port of Smyrna in Asia Minor. Holbrook's *B11* was on patrol there on 17 May when von Voigt was forced to take the *UB8* in with compass trouble, and was actually sighted as the U-boat steamed in.

10.0 am. Sighted hostile submarine, apparently on motors about 4 miles from me proceeding towards Smyrna and very close inshore. She looked very much like one of our later E boats with a straight bow and more superstructure forward than aft, and with a conical-shaped conning tower. I dived immediately to attack her. At 10.30 I came to the surface and discovered she was under way at full speed on her engines, with a large bow wave. On sighting me she dived. I never saw her again.

Holbrook had hopelessly overestimated the size of the enemy submarine but nevertheless this was the first sighting of one of these new boats, and proof that there was now another menace to be faced by the warships attacking the Dardanelles.

With reports that the Germans were establishing a base at Bodrum, allied submarines were sent to the vicinity to keep watch. This was a task for both the older British B-class and also for the French boats. The *B10* (Lieutenant S. M. G. Gravener) carried out the first such patrol from 16 April to 5 May in company with the converted minesweeper *HMS Gazelle*, another ex-railway ferry. (Immediately after this episode the *Gazelle* underwent another conversion to become a minelayer and then laid the first British minefield off Smyrna, which might account for the loss of the *UB3*.) For nearly three weeks the two ships kept a fruitless watch on the port, an unheard-of time on patrol for such an old submarine whose prewar limit had been considered as three days, even allowing for the somewhat unconventional manner in which the operation was conducted and for the support given to the submarine by the ex-ferry. Whenever possible the submarine lay alongside the *Gazelle* overnight, proceeding to her day position an hour before daylight.

21 April.
   I observed Karada Island to be uninhabited except for two farms on the NE side and decided to lie off the SE shore of the island so as to be able to carry out a more efficient patrol of Bodrum during daylight. I laid out small moorings 600 yards from the shore in a position so that the lookout could see the Channel between Kos and the Dorian Promontory and between Kos and the mainland to the SE. I lay at these moorings during daylight. Before proceeding to the rendezvous [with the GAZELLE] I steamed into Bodrum harbour and examined it.

26 April
   9.0 am. I landed with the Coxswain, both armed, and climbed to the top of Karada and examined Bodrum harbour, returning at noon.

Such a landing party became a regular feature of Gravener's time off Bodrum, but before the end of the patrol they were fired on. A search of the island revealed no signs of an enemy landing party, but the next day two local peasants from one of the farms, obviously overexcited by the sight of strangers, came to the shore with a white flag to make their peace. They came out to the submarine offering a live goat and a large cheese. Gravener's report fails to mention how he dealt with either of these gifts, neither of which were very suitable for the confines of a small submarine.

Despite these patrols the arrival of the *UB7* at Bodrum on 20 May went unobserved. Werner went on to Smyrna, arriving there on the last day of the month where the submarine stayed until the middle of June when she sailed direct for Constantinople.

Meanwhile von Voigt had sailed from Smyrna with the *UB8* early on the 29th, again undetected. Despite the large number of ships now in the Eastern Mediterranean he had not sighted any targets until dusk on the 30th, when a large three-funnelled ship was sighted proceeding towards Mudros. Von Voigt fired one torpedo with which he claimed a hit abreast the after funnel, but there is no record of this attack in British records. He entered the Dardanelles on 2 June and headed towards Constantinople. Of course, he faced few of the difficulties that were presented to Stoker, Boyle and Nasmith. Once clear of any British patrols he was able to surface and make his way carefully up a marked route under the protection of the guns of the Turkish forts.

Yet, not unexpectedly, it was Hersing in the *U21* that had the greatest success. He had sailed from Cattaro on the evening of 20 May. On the 24th he sighted the Russian cruiser *Askold*, with her distinctive five funnels and known to the British troops as 'The Packet of Woodbines'. She was lying at anchor and it looked to be a chance that he could not miss, yet he decided not to attack, saving both his torpedoes and the element of surprise for when he came upon the main Anglo-French fleet. The following day was windless, the sea a flat calm and the visibility excellent when Hersing sighted his target off Cape Helles. Perhaps it was too calm for not only did he miss, having fired a single torpedo at each of the two battleships *Swiftsure* and *Vengeance* but his periscope was sighted close to them. An officer in the *Swiftsure* later described the scene:

> I was dressing, about 7.30 am, when I heard shouts followed by the rapid firing of guns. I rushed to the quarterdeck to ascertain the cause for the alarm. A sailor told me that he had seen the periscope of a submarine appear within 300 yards of us. The crew had immediately opened fire with the 14-pounders on the unwelcome intruder, who appears to have been thoroughly scared and dived for safety. The submarine certainly missed the chance of a lifetime, because, in addition to the SWIFTSURE, the AGAMEMNON was lying within 100 yards, and the old MAJESTIC a

short distance further off. Probably the submarine came up "blind" and was fired upon before she had time to lay on a target. This proof of the enemy's presence caused fresh consternation throughout the fleet, and no one seemed to know what the next move would be. The AGAMEMNON received orders to weight anchor, and go back to Mudros, as she was too valuable a ship to risk. It is uncomfortable lying at anchor knowing that at any moment you may be blown to smithereens by an unseen foe. It is not so bad when the ship is under way, as you feel you have a chance, but here we lay presenting a 'sitter' to the sportsman mean enough to take advantage of such a target.

The *U21* crept away and a few hours later found the *Triumph* at anchor with her anti-torpedo nets out and a destroyer slowly circling her. Hersing fired one torpedo. Despite the nets there was no doubt as to the result. The battleship slowly heeled over and in half an hour was gone. The same officer in the *Swiftsure* again records the events that followed:

We then adjourned for lunch, and had nearly finished, when a young signalman came to the commander with cap in hand, and said, with a most apologetic air for interrupting his meal, 'Beg pardon, sir, the TRIUMPH is listing'. We rushed on deck, where every officer was assembled, and there sure enough lay the unfortunate battleship with a heavy list and stricken to death. Destroyers were rushing to her assistance, almost covering the horizon with dense clouds of black smoke. Fortunately there was a trawler close to the TRIUMPH at the time, which was able to take off a number of her crew. The battleship hung at an angle of about forty-five degrees for about eight minutes and then turned bottom upwards, floating in this position for twenty minutes, looking like a whale at rest.

The sight was greeted with consternation in the Australian trenches nearby for the *Triumph's* guns had given them good support in the previous few days. Only yards away in the Turkish trenches there was unbounded delight.

Hersing claims that the destroyers hunted him determinedly and that he only escaped by taking the *U21* under the sinking *Triumph*, though it may well be that much of the activity was caused by the destroyers rushing to the battleship's aid. Nevertheless Hersing deemed it prudent to remain dived until nightfall.

The following day he attempted to find the *Askold*, but by then she was no longer at her anchorage. On the 27th he had another success. Again he fired a single torpedo which again found its mark through a protective ring of destroyers and anti-submarine nets. This time the target was the battleship *Majestic*, which capsized and sank within minutes.

> The MAJESTIC presented an extrordinary spectacle. She was lying over on her side, having such a list that it was no longer possible to stand on her deck. About one-third of her crew still seemed to be hanging on to the rails or clinging to her side, as if hesitating to jump into the water. All round the sea was full of men, some swimming towards neighbouring ships, others apparently having their work cut out to keep themselves afloat. All the vessels in the neighbourhood were lowering boats, and steam launches were hastening to pick up survivors, but they did not dare stand in too close for fear of being dragged under in the final plunge. I was just thinking what a magnificent photograph the scene would make, when the MAJESTIC rolled right over to port and sank bottom upwards like a great stone, without any further warning. There came a great rumbling sound, a swirl of water and steam, for a moment her green bottom was exposed to view, and then the old flagship disappeared for ever, except for a small piece of her ram, which remained above water as her bows were lying on a shallow sandbank. As she turned over and sank a sailor ran the whole length of her keel and finally sat astride the ram from where he was taken off without even getting a wetting. The final plunge was so inspiring that for a few seconds I forgot about the large number of officers and men who were still clinging to her like limpets when she went down.

These losses following the destruction of the *Goliath* in the middle of the month, which had been torpedoed and sunk by the Turkish torpedo boat *Muavenet*, the heavy units of the fleet were all withdrawn from the area. It was a bad blow for the morale of the British and Australian troops who no longer had the comfort of the heavy guns of the battleships to support them. It left Hersing with no more worthwhile targets and he too headed for Constantinople.

Nasmith kept the *E11* in the Sea of Marmara until 7 June at which stage a defect on the port main motor made a return imperative. Throughout this period Nasmith made his presence felt, ensuring that the Turks were reluctant to move supplies by sea. He was hampered only by a shortage of torpedoes and, as with Boyle and the *E14*, the lack of a gun. Two particular episodes stick out among the many of this long and successful patrol.

On the very day that Hersing was making a name for himself off Cape Helles Nasmith took the *E11* to the heart of the Turkish Empire, into the harbour of Constantinople. By this time he had only one of his periscopes still useable, the other having been damaged by a lucky shot from a Turkish destroyer, but coming to periscope depth inside the harbour he sighted a large transport lying at the jetty in the arsenal. Nearby to him was the American cruiser acting as guardship for their Embassy, the Stars and Stripes at her stern boldly proclaiming her neutrality. The first torpedo fired failed to run properly and Nasmith was forced to fire a second. Then, to his horror, the first torpedo circled round and came back towards the *E11* and he was forced to go deep to avoid becoming his own victim. In doing so he missed the explosion as the second, running straight and true, hit the transport. Where the first torpedo finally exploded Nasmith never knew, but it could have only just missed the American ship, and who knows what the consequences might have been had the cruiser been sunk by a British torpedo?

The actual effect of this one torpedo was not enough to sink the transport, but the moral effect of the explosion was more pronounced for it was plain to all in the heart of this great metropolis. While the ship was only holed and did not sink, the troops on board had to be disembarked and begin a long weary march to the front. It was a march that was to become routine for Turkish reinforcements on their way to the front as the effect of the British submarines became more marked on Turkish shipping in the Sea of Marmara as the months went by.

Nasmith's great worry was the limited number of torpedoes that he could carry. There was only one answer. He would have to find a way to re-use any that were fired and failed to hit or to explode. The torpedoes were therefore set to float rather than sink at the end of their run, then the *E11* could surface as soon as it was safe to do so and look for the errant weapon. The first time they tried this Nasmith himself swam out to unscrew the firing pistol – an operation akin to defusing a bomb while swimming. The torpedo was then floated into the stern torpedo tube of the submarine. The submarine was then trimmed bow down so that the outer door of the tube was clear of the water and the torpedo could be hauled into the boat, a very dangerous procedure since it meant having both inner and outer doors open at the same time and the submarine unable to dive quickly should the enemy be sighted. There was then the task of preparing the torpedo for a second run. This is easier said than done for the 17-foot-long weapon had first to be broken down into its component sections, the more easy to handle them in the confined space of the submarine. Re-assembled, tested, recharged and reprimed it could then be loaded into one of the forward tubes for another run. It was a daunting task, as any submariner can testify, yet it was done in hostile waters and done successfully. And done again too.

Even the *E11's* return trip through the Dardanelles was fraught with incident. The submarine caught a mine and towed it through the Strait with her, luckily the black ball of death floated clear of the submarine's conning tower. Surfacing at the southern end of the Straits would be the dangerous time when the mine could so easily strike the submarine with one of its sensitive horns. Nasmith got over this problem by going astern as he brought the *E11* to the surface leaving the mine to break free and disappear into the depths clear of the bows of the submarine. Like Boyle before him, Nasmith received the VC and his crew were also decorated.

10

The New Venture

THE *E7*, WITH Cochrane and Hallifax, in company with the *E12*,
arrived in Devonport at midday on 30 May, a Sunday. Life in
Devonport was very different from the hustle and bustle which was
commonplace at Harwich where the destroyers and submarines were
constantly going to and from patrol, and were frequently in action
with the enemy. In November, 1914, there had been the excitement at
Devonport of getting Vice-Admiral Sturdee's two battlecruisers
ready for sea as they rushed off to meet the German Squadron at the
Falkland Islands. But that was now in the past, and, war or no war,
Sunday was a day of rest in Devonport.

The two submarines berthed on the *Sarnia*, a 1500-ton ex-ferry of
the London and South-West Railway Company built in 1910 and now
taken into the Navy. Since the early days of the war she had been used
for contraband control but now was to accompany the two submarines
out to the Dardanelles taking with her extra stores and spare gear.

Having all our meals in SARNIA; her officers are all RNR, crew RNR and
RNVR except the stokers, trimmers and stewards who are all originals and
signed on for six months. The trouble is that the six months are up and half
of them refuse to re-engage. One of the engineers is round at Southampton
trying to collect a crew.

The head steward of the SARNIA is a most friendly old man, and the
way he hovers tenderly round one urging one to have some more soup or
something at meals makes me feel like an invalid returning from death's
door being tended by some perfectly devoted friend.

At this time Boyle was already back from his first patrol in the Sea of

Marmara and had concluded his report with a plea for a gun to be fitted to submarines going on patrol. Nasmith was already near the end of his patrol and he too was acutely aware of the limitations forced on the submarine's Commanding Officer by the small number of torpedoes that a submarine could carry on patrol and by the lack of a gun to use on small targets. The *E7* and the *E12* were both earmarked to be fitted with a gun, but there seemed no sense of urgency to get the work done before they sailed again.

> Cochrane and I went round to the Constructor's office to ask if the pad for our gun could be fitted tomorrow. He took the greatest trouble to make arrangements, being unable to put anyone on the job today – there is no work here on a Sunday unless very pressing – and fixed it all up for tomorrow.

> *31 May*
> At 6.30 pm the gun pad still had two more holes to drill and only four screwed bolts in place which meant 12 holes in our upper deck! Shoved off and secured to a buoy off Drake's Island and at 8 o'clock the Dockyard fitters arrived with bolts and temporarily bolted up the holes.

The *Sarnia* and the two submarines slipped away from the Sound and into the Channel at 11 o'clock that night. The sailing had had to be delayed to allow the *Sarnia* to complete her crew, and even then she had to sail short-handed. With the *E7* on *E12's* quarter and the *Sarnia* out to port the small group set course to pass 50 miles off Ushant and then down through the Bay of Biscay well clear of the usual shipping routes. Even so they did sight some ships and one liner altered course to put as much distance as possible between her and the submarines, just to be on the safe side. The weather failed to live up to its Biscayan reputation and remained fine and calm for the entire passage to Gibraltar. For the submariners it was an unusual experience after months on patrol in the Heligoland Bight; they were on the surface all the time, there were no mines to worry about, the weather became warmer and warmer as they went south and, above all, they were untroubled about meeting the enemy, though this may have been unwise for it was not so long previously that Hersing had taken the *U21* that way.

> *3 June.* (Off the Spanish coast)
> When working in the North Sea I did not think much about mines after

the first trip or two, at least I had that impression, but now crossing a lovely calm blue sea with no mines, enemy ships or aircraft to worry about I realize how much one did think of them. Its perfectly glorious to be able to feel that there is nothing to worry about. The sun felt very different this morning when I went on deck at 8 o'clock, and I shed my coat and sweater during the forenoon watch.

They arrived in Gibraltar on the evening of the 4th, stayed little more then 12 hours to fuel, clean up and hear the latest news and then left for Malta. Again the weather was kind, the sea smooth with barely a ripple. Their progress was marred only by breakdowns to the *E12's* engines, and then, with Malta almost in sight, the *E7* had to stop one engine for repairs to be made. As a result of these delays they arrived too late to enter harbour for the night and anchored in St Paul's Bay, entering Grand Harbour early on the 9th.

Entered Grand Harbour astern of SARNIA. There were two big liners, one the IVERNIA, in Bighi Bay, the latter with 1200 wounded from the Dardanelles on board and the other full of troops on their way out. The harbour was full of French battleships, destroyers and half a dozen submarines. Went alongside a cruiser under Fort St Angelo outside the E12. Ahead of the cruiser was a French transport, the TROUVILLE, acting as a depot ship for the submarines. Alongside her was our old friend the ARCHIMEDE, with the GUSTAVE ZEDE and one other. The GUSTAVE ZEDE is a horrible looking affair with a very high casing in which the crew lives.

They were to spend a few days resting in Malta while the Dockyard carried out work on the two boats. In the event it was hardly restful for the *E7's* engine-room staff for Cochrane decided that he did not want the Dockyard to work on the engines fearing that their lack of knowledge and experience might make things worse rather than better. It was not a popular move as the temperature in the submarine's engine room rose higher and higher in the unaccustomed heat of a Maltese summer. The *E12* were happy to have the Dockyard work for them. The Dockyard did finish off fitting the pad for the *E7's* gun, and they also bolted down the pedestal, though it was not to be a straightforward task.

Found that the Dockyard had failed us with a boat for our gun, so in desperation got a cutter from the cruiser and with four men pulled over to the SARNIA to collect it ourselves. There I found only the gun on deck with the other parts in the hold, and they took some while to get up. At length we got them all over to the submarine and whipped the pedestal up into place. As the Maltese shoved the bolts in we hoisted the mounting and the gun into position in great style.

The two submarines and the *Sarnia* found their time in Malta all too short and when they came to leave on the morning of 12 June the *E7's* engines were still not ready. Cochrane was eager to press on and sailed with his consorts despite this handicap. The crew had one engine ready as they passed the famous Fort St Elmo at the harbour entrance and the other was not ready for use until some three hours later.

The Engine Room hands are absolutely done up for they have been working continuously since we arrived and the heat in the Engine Room has been terrible. I wish we could have had another day so as to get it properly finished and give the hands a night in.

The weather on passage was very hot, making conditions on board uncomfortable. In an attempt to keep the boat cool they spread the bridge awning, which made some difference down below but would not have helped them much had they had to dive in a hurry on meeting one of the U-boats then present in the Mediterranean. They did meet one old friend, sighting the *E11* going back under tow to Malta to refit at the end of her first famous patrol in the Marmara. Cochrane himself seemed to resent the time taken to reach the Eastern Mediterranean and would pore over the chart as if willing the miles away. He had grudged putting into Gibraltar as a waste of half a day and Hallifax had been rather surprised at the time allowed in Malta, although, as has been seen, it was time well spent on refitting the engines.

Two days out from Malta they reached the island of Lemnos with its great natural harbour of Mudros. After answering the challenge of a patrolling destroyer they turned towards the entrance and made their way through the gate in the net defences. After rounding Sangrada Point, where Stoker and the *AE2* had gone so embarassingly aground, they were able to head for their berth alongside the *Adamant*.

Mudros was an amazing sight. Numerous battleships and other warships were anchored in long lines as if for review. Troop transports and supply ships were unloading new supplies and reinforcements for the army while the hospital ships were present to take the wounded away to Malta and 'Blighty'. Ashore the lines of the many tented camps broke up the bleak arid landscape while the troops themselves raised clouds of dust as they marched around the island in 'columns of fours'. It was hot, dirty and insanitary. Dead mules floated in the harbour, their long legs sticking forlornly into the air like so many periscopes.

19 June
It is getting hotter every day and the ADAMANT is undoubtedly the hottest ship ever built. Her odd shape prevents any breeze being felt anywhere but on the bridge.

23 June
I was violently sick last night and have come to the conclusion it was caused by the heat and a slight touch of the sun. Wore a helmet this afternoon on deck and my green glasses when I landed for a bathe. Felt quite well again this evening. Terrifically hot and the mess is almost unbearable. We dine on deck every evening and I always sleep on deck.

24 June
I started a new routine this morning. We start work in the boat at 5 o'clock, go to breakfast from 7.30 to 8.15, and then work to noon and finish. No work is done in the boat – if possible – in the afternoon which is so frightfully hot here. The stokers and the ERAs much prefer this routine but I don't think that the seamen like it!

On 10 June, just three days after Nasmith's safe return with the *E11* from the Sea of Marmara, Boyle had successfully navigated the Straits for a second time in the *E14*. This time the submarine was additionally armed with a 6-pounder gun. It was just as well for there were few targets to be found which warranted the expenditure of a torpedo, for the Turks had begun carrying their supplies to Gallipoli in a variety of sailing craft and even in lighters towed by tugs, and frequently escorted by destroyers and gunboats. Despite this Boyle maintained a steady stream of successes, the Turks never knowing from one day to the next when or where this elusive submarine would turn up. He was to remain in the Sea of Marmara for twenty-three days.

Nine days after Boyle's passage up the Dardanelles he was followed into the Sea of Marmara by the *E12*, with Lieutenant-Commander K. Bruce being chosen, much to Cochrane's chagrin, to be the first of the newcomers to attempt the passage.

They had to start diving on the way up earlier than expected as the French opened fire on them from their lines. Soon afterwards they ran aground at 80 feet and then fetched up with the conning tower out of the water. Not knowing which side they might be Fox [the First Lieutenant] went on deck and found the northern cliffs towering over him. They ran aground once more. They were little troubled and no fire was opened on them by the Turks during the passage.

The *E12*'s patrol was short as she had defects first on one motor and then on the other. She was ordered to return before further trouble which might have prevented any dived passage at all, and she safely reached Mudros again on the 27th, entering harbour flying a red flag with a skull and crossbones on it. This signal of success had first been flown by the *E9* when Horton returned to Harwich after sinking the German cruiser *Hela*, and it was to become a universal tradition amongst British and allied submariners during the Second World War.

The *E12* had had one particularly unpleasant experience when dealing with a steamer which had been towing two sailing vessels. The steamer was small, two-decked and described by Bruce as looking rather like a small tram. With the steamer stopped, the submarine steamed slowly round her and Bruce could see that all the crew appeared to be on deck wearing their lifebelts. He thought that it might be carrying stores and as he could not see a gun he ran his bow alongside so that his First Lieutenant and a couple of ratings could go on board. As the boarding party was about to step on board someone threw a bomb at the submarine which luckily did not explode. Fortunately the gun was loaded and there were rifles ready on the conning tower and fire was immediately opened on the steamer, the first shot being aimed at a small gun aft which had been uncovered and had opened fire on the submarine. They had put ten shots into her when she exploded, as her cargo of ammunition was hit, and sank about fifteen minutes later. Rifle fire had also been aimed at the submarine from the two sailing craft and they tried to foul the submarine's propellors as she went clear. They too were sunk. Miraculously only one of the submarine's crew was mildly wounded.

A second steamer, also with two other vessels in tow, had been sighted closer inshore at the same time as the first one had been engaged. Bruce now went to engage that and opened fire at about 1500 yards' range, driving the ship ashore. During this brief action the submarine was fired at from ashore, but Bruce retired from the scene without damage.

The E12's motor broke down on the first day in the Marmara. Then the other motor failed and could only be used "Grouper Down" [slow speeds], so they came back down the Dardanelles on one motor only in this way. At one time they started turning round and round and thought that they had been caught by something, but discovered finally that it was the result of having so little way on and the current being with them (eddies too I expect).

With the news that the *E12* was returning, it was time for the *E7* to make all the final preparations to take her place. For Cochrane there was to be the chance to fly over the Straits so that he could see what lay ahead for him. While he was airborne the aircraft developed engine trouble and the pilot was forced to return with only half the reconnaissance completed.

Saturday 26 June.
Busy day; unshipped all bridge stanchions, dismantled the gun which we lashed on deck and the mounting which we dropped into the casing, took in provisions for a month and filled up with water. Charged the battery right up.

More important to their future efficiency, several of the crew were suffering from dysentery, brought about no doubt by the general conditions prevailing in Mudros. Another rating fell badly and hurt his side but was most anxious not to be left behind, the doctor eventually heeding his pleas. Hallifax himself had had one attack of dysentery but by this time had recovered.

29 June
The three men with dysentery are joining up again today for I pointed out to the doctor that they would probably recover as soon as we get away from here, for the general opinion is that the flies are the cause of it. Ships in other parts of the harbour do not get infected as much as we do. We think that they come from the slaughterhouse which is just opposite us on the water's edge.

So the *E7* was ready for her attempt at entering the Sea of Marmara to relieve Boyle, still there on his second patrol. At 7.30 pm on 29 June

Cochrane took the *E7* away from her berth on the *Adamant* and out to sea heading towards the Dardanelles, while a disconsolate Bruce took the *E12* to Malta for repairs. As the submarines left a vicious north-westerly squall burst around the harbour accompanied by brilliant forked lightning all round the horizon. Some might have regarded this as a sign of trouble to come for the Turks.

I hear that when the *E14* last reported herself the other day she said that there were few targets now in the Marmara; bad lookout for us. However, Cochrane is full of ideas, and we ought to do something!

11

The Sea Of Marmara

WEDNESDAY 30 JUNE, 3.30 am: Hallifax climbed excitedly to the bridge as the *E7* made steady progress northwards. The rain that earlier had marked the submarine's departure from Mudros had ceased, while the wind which had been quite strong had died away to a gentle breeze. The night sky was lit by lightning around the horizon. Over to port the white cliffs of Cape Helles showed starkly where the natural effects of the storm were enhanced as the gun flashes flickered over the tip of the peninsula and occasional flares shot into the sky, fired no doubt by some nervous sentry to illuminate the front before him. To starboard the searchlight at Kum Kale shed its powerful beam over the waters, while futher up the Straits the beams of other searchlights could be seen marking both shores like so many navigational beacons. The sound of the guns could be heard above the steady beat of the engines and the swish of the water along the submarine's ballast tanks. Overhead could be heard the express-train roar of a heavy shell on its way towards the British trenches as a Turkish battery on the Asiatic shore fired steadily.

Hallifax had little time to appreciate the scene for hardly had he reached the bridge than Cochrane ordered 'Diving Stations' and he had to go below again. Twenty minutes later and some four miles up the Straits Cochrane judged that the time had come to dive and the *E7* slid down gently to 80 feet. Cochrane brought them back to periscope depth from time to time to check their position, otherwise they made steady but blind progress up the Straits relying on Twyman's dead reckoning. What Hallifax did not realize was that Cochrane was ill, probably too ill to have gone on with wisdom, but driven to do so by his own fierce determination. He later admitted that he had felt so ill that he was contemplating returning when the *E7* went aground off Nagara and that by the time he had sorted that out he had forgotten his intention!

> He told me that he could scarcely see through the periscope and had apparently told Twyman to see that he did nothing silly. When he came to periscope depth he took three bearings which he called out to Twyman and then went to 80 feet again. Twyman was then told to go forward and stay there. Cochrane merely moved the ruler over the chart without any pencil marks, then folded up his chart and sat on it. He took two more fixes in this manner with Twyman kept well away. It was only later he told us that the bearings were shams for he could not see anything clearly! Its this infernal diarrhoea or dysentery. Twyman had it too and was pretty bad for a while.

At noon they were through, breaking surface off the town of Gallipoli. They had had one exciting moment when a gunboat, having sighted their periscope, had come at them at full speed. With rare humour Cochrane described the scene with the submarine, all too close to the steep shore, going to 40 feet to allow the enemy to pass over and then, hopefully, going aground.

Having got through the Straits Cochrane took the *E7* to the bottom to wait for dark when they could surface. Most of the crew went to sleep, few bothered to eat. Shortly before 9 o'clock the welcome order passed through the boat; the air was foul after so long a dive, the inside of the hull was dripping with condensation and the batteries had very little power left. Gently the boat was brought to 20 feet for Cochrane to search the horizon for the enemy before surfacing. Hallifax was the first out of the conning tower into the fresh air and was surprised to find the land apparently so close on either side, the Marmara being less than ten miles across at this point, and in the clear night air the shores looked even closer. They then set about recharging the submarine's batteries ready to begin operations.

The Sea of Marmara may be regarded as a box some 150 miles long from east to west and about 40 miles in breadth at its widest part from north to south, lying between the Black Sea and the Aegean. At the western end for about 30 miles eastward from the town of Gallipoli it narrows in width to between 3 and 10 miles before entering the Dardanelles which join it to the Aegean. On the northern shore lies the city of Constantinople, which with its twin Scutari, lies astride the

Bosphorus linking the Marmara with the Black Sea. For most of its area the sea is deep, about 950 feet, with surprisingly gentle sloping beaches. It is bordered almost throughout its length by high mountainous country with many small towns dotted along its shores. There were few good roads in the area, and fewer railways, increasing the importance, indeed the necessity, for travel by sea. In the centre lies the Island of Marmara which gives its name to the sea.

At 7.30 the following morning, 1 July, they sighted their first target, a small two-funnelled steamer, and hastened to close and intercept. As they got closer she proved to be a hospital ship and she had to be allowed to proceed. After that the sea was empty of shipping and they spent the morning mounting and testing the gun while in the afternoon they met up with the *E14*. Cochrane went across to see Boyle while the latter's First Lieutenant came across to talk to Hallifax. All four officers exchanged news and information before returning to their own boats and parting to go their own ways.

The following morning the *E7* was off the port of Rodosto, on the north shore of the Marmara some 55 miles from Constantinople and 35 miles north of the Island of Marmara. The town itself was prosperous-looking and picturesque, the houses being built on the slopes of a hill running gently down to the bay where a number of storehouses marked the waterfront. But they were not there to admire the beauty of the scene, rather to deal with the shipping in the area – a steamer and five sailing vessels. The hospital ship they had sighted the day previously was also seen, this time going eastwards and obviously well filled. The water shoals gradually off the town and the ships had gone as close inshore as they dared, hoping no doubt to deter any action by the by now well known British submarines and where they might gain some protection from the troops in the area. As soon as the *E7* was seen one of the schooners ran aground, while two others who had their sails furled and the crews ashore could do nothing.

Carefully Cochrane closed the shore, for the last thing he wanted was to go aground himself, and headed towards the steamer at anchor. Some Turkish troops opened fire with their rifles but the range was too great. Twyman said afterwards that he had heard the sounds of gunfire but only one tired bullet had plopped into the water nearby. One round from the submarine's gun had caused consternation and the troops ashore had retired out of range. Hallifax was told to prepare a scuttling charge and while doing so was told by Cochrane to bring a tin of petrol to the bridge as he did not wish to waste too much time. He would then use the charge on the brigantine after Hallifax and Able Seaman Mathews had set the steamer on fire.

> We jumped on board and went down the focsle ladder. At the foot of the ladder on each side was a door leading into a little cabin with a mattress on each bunk. There were plenty of wicker baskets lying around so we jammed them on the bunks and poured some petrol on each mattress. Not having had anything to do with petrol for so long now I forgot how it vapourises and thought of it as paraffin, and having sent Mathews on deck with the half-empty can I told him when he returned to light his side and then nip on deck, and I would light mine and follow him.
>
> The compartment we were in was quite small. He lit his match and leant forward and there was a blinding flash and the air seemed to burst into flame.

Both men were badly burnt. Mathews was burnt on the face, neck, forearms and hands. Hallifax had the side of his right forearm burnt raw and both feet and legs up to the calves were raw and blistered. Even so they scrambled to safety from the burning ship, momentarily sticking in a doorway as they both tried to get through together, and being guided below in the submarine to get their injuries attended to. But what to do? There was no doctor on board but inevitably there was no shortage of advice.

> Everyone said oil so the large case of sperm oil was brought along and poured over us and lint soaked in it was place on our wounds. Then Sims [Petty Officer] appeared and said that picric lint was the stuff and put that on instead. The constant wetting of this stuff had a soothing effect. While being soused with oil I began to feel faint so got hold of a bottle of Sal Volatile. Thinking there was not time to find if this had to be diluted, for no one there knew, of that I am certain, I poured a third of a wine glass and tossed it off! It stopped me fainting but am sure it must have nearly killed me for I couldn't breathe or do anything but glare at the bottle and signal for water. When that came I drank two big tumblers full to drown it.

Meanwhile the steamer was burning merrily and a couple of shells on the waterline hastened her end as the scuttling charge had blown the nearby brigantine to pieces. Another brigantine was sunk by gunfire. Cochrane's hopes of sinking all the ships were dashed by the arrival of a Turkish gunboat which forced the *E7* to dive.

The following day another brigantine was captured, the Greek crew being watched over by a very ancient Turkish soldier – 95 was Twyman's estimate of his age. Nevertheless, whatever his age or martial ability, he had wisely thrown his rifle overboard before the British boarding party arrived. Ordering the Greeks into the ship's boat, the submariners again tried their hands at arson. Their first attempts with petrol were failures and they were lucky not to repeat the disaster of the previous day, but a couple of gallons of paraffin soon solved the problem and the brigantine was left burning fiercely. The Greeks were towed towards the shore, a kindly act which had to be ended with the arrival yet again of a gunboat. On board the *E7* the condition of the two injured men was causing Cochrane considerable concern and he had resolved to send them back with Boyle in the *E14* if he should be met with again. It was not to be.

Whilst dived Cochrane examined my feet and legs and they were a horrid sight – covered with huge blisters like Portuguese men-of-war. The arm which was raw he washed again and bound with boric lint. Looking at my feet I thought that the blisters would heal in a week and I should be able to move about in a fortnight at the most, but Cochrane had not taken the bandage right off but just looked inside. I did not hurt much then, not enough to prevent me sleeping.

4 July
I lie on the upper bunk all day and climb onto the lower one for meals. Yesterday I had meals at the table but this dysentery business has started again and I only have soup, biscuits and tea now with some vegetables at lunch.

5 July
I now suffer torture when I have to use my feet. As a matter of fact I sort of swing along from pipe to pipe and beam to beam with only my heels touching the deck. When I have to stand on my feet it makes me sweat with pain.

The sick list on board the *E7* did not end with the badly burnt Hallifax and Mathews. Both Cochrane and Twyman and several of the crew were suffering with constant diarrhoea and for two days little work was done while Cochrane kept the submarine out of sight. Luckily the trouble cleared itself in all but one rating – the only Telegraphist on board, Albert Parodi – where the illness developed into acute dysentery. In turn this meant that Leading Signalman

Reggie Hooper, whose duties and training were in visual signalling and who knew little of the mysteries of wireless, had to operate the set. With the submarine in the western end of the Sea of Marmara they were meant to send messages via the destroyer HMS *Jed*, lying across the Gallipoli peninsula in the Gulf of Xeros, who in turn would relay the signals to Mudros. Hooper, working in unaccustomed conditions, was unable to make contact with the *Jed*, and finally just broadcast his messages hoping they would be picked up. What neither he nor Cochrane knew was that they were being heard perfectly by the destroyer, but were unable to receive the signals meant for them. In this way did Keyes come to hear that Cochrane had successfully navigated the Dardanelles and had begun his campaign against the Turkish supply line running down the Sea of Marmara, following in the style already set by Boyle and Nasmith.

Meanwhile Parodi's condition added to Cochrane's other worries and the strain of operating the *E7* in such confined waters.

He has eaten nothing for days and yet strains every minutes and passes blood. They have tried a hot flannel but he yelled and could not stand it. He got weaker and weaker and the smell around him must have been awful for the crew but they were all very good to him except young Levey (Ordinary Signalman) who sneered at Parodi and if the latter asked him to do something for him merely told him to turn out and get it himself.

One evening Twyman, who knows a lot about dysentery for he has been in tankers in the Persian Gulf, told Cochrane and me that he did not think Parodi would live another day. He wished we had some oil for Parodi to drink, and Cochrane had the bright idea of using strained sardine oil. He poured out a wine glass full and strained it through a silk hankerchief of mine – though why I should have brought one with me I can't think! He told Parodi to sip the oil and it soothed him at once and he drank the lot. Next day he was free of pain and started eating ravenously and was able to leave his hammock. A day or two later the curtain opposite my bunk drew apart and what looked like a skull looked at me. In the state I was in I nearly screamed.

Daily the toll of small shipping sunk or damaged by the *E7* rose. There was the dhow–like vessel being towed by what appeared to be a large motor yacht; when the submarine drew near they were surprised when the yacht slipped her tow and opened fire from concealed guns, probably 3-pounders. The submarine returned fire as the yacht made off, but only managed one hit before the helm jammed at a vital moment and, as the submarine continued to turn, the gun would no longer bear. The dhow was sunk when Cochrane had sorted things out. A ferry was chased and run ashore. She was left apparently sinking with two shotholes on the waterline, only for the same vessel to be met again the next day. There was no second chance and she was sunk in deep water. One of the *E7's* precious torpedoes was fired at a destroyer escorting some tugs towing a string of dhows and lighters, but though a satisfying explosion was heard this was the torpedo hitting the beach rather than its target. Despite the number of destroyers and gunboats with which the Turks patrolled the Sea of Marmara Cochrane continued to be able to sink the small craft and ferries which were so essential a part of communications between the capital and the forces at the front on the Gallipoli peninsula.

Just after dawn on 10 July Cochrane brought the *E7* for a second time into the Gulf of Mudania towards the port of the same name. Lying alongside the only jetty was a 3–4,000 ton steamer partly protected by several sailing vessels which were lying alongside and into which she was discharging her cargo. A torpedo was fired from about 1500 yards' range at the exposed after end of the ship and they were rewarded with a satisfying explosion – the first successful torpedo attack by the *E7*. Cochrane reported that a column of water was thrown about 300 feet into the air and the ship broke in two by the mainmast.

The *E7* withdrew to seaward after this attack and, finding a quiet spot where Cochrane hoped they would be out of sight, celebrated by allowing hands to bathe. It was not just an attempt at recreation but had the serious purpose of allowing the crew to have a decent wash. Even Hallifax was able to take the opportunity of some fresh air, and presumably Mathews too, though Hallifax makes no mention of this in his diary.

> I put on flannel trousers and a shirt and got helped up the fore hatch on to a chair on the casing. I ought to have got another chair to put my feet on as they don't like the sitting postion when all the blood runs down to them. I had to wear my green glasses to prevent being blinded in the bright sun after so long in artificial light. I did envy the men washing and bathing.

Eventually they were discovered by a patrolling gunboat and forced to get the swimmers on board, shut all the hatches again and then dive to safety. Cochrane's report merely stated 'Gunboat interrupted the proceedings while ventilating and washing clothes,' but made no mention of his own justifiable annoyance for it was his turn to bathe next!

By this time the Turks were using mostly small craft to take both troops and supplies to Gallipoli, which is indicative of the effect of the British submarine campaign. Large transports were considered unsafe and rarely used.

Instead of a short sea trip many Turkish soldiers were faced with a roundabout train journey followed by a march of at least five days south into the peninsula. For the bullock carts and camels carrying the supplies it meant a considerably longer period on the road. Such was the measure of the success of the submarines.

13 July – though a Tuesday not a Friday – began badly for Cochrane. Having spent yet another night at the western end of the Marmara trying in vain to establish two-way wireless communication with the *Jed*, he turned the *E7* towards Karabuga Bay before dawn. Karabuga was a small port standing at one end of the bay, fringed by a sandy beach and served by a single jetty. The port supplied a much larger town several miles inland and Cochrane hoped that it would be a fruitful area for attacking local shipping.

At 8 o'clock they sighted what was first thought to be at least a monitor or even one of the Turkish Navy's old battleships, but was later identified as the old gunboat *Muni-i-Zaffer* which had been launched as long ago as 1869 and was then armed with four 5.9 inch guns and even carried the old-fashioned ram on the bow. Just as Cochrane was ready to fire the helmsman wandered off course, then applied the helm the wrong way and before the mistake could be remedied they were aground on the soft mud. By the time Cochrane had worked the submarine free the *Muni-i-Zaffer* was already leaving the harbour escorting two small steamers, all blissfully unaware of their lucky escape. Luck continued to favour the Turks, for yet another error on board left Cochrane unable to use even his stern tube before the small convoy was out of range. There was still a cluster of small ships lying alongside the jetty and grimly Cochrane ordered a torpedo to be fired. It ran true and exploded among the ships causing some damage, but just how much they were unable to assess. In any event it did something – but not much – to mollify an angry Cochrane. The *Muni-i-Zaffer* sailed on to survive the war and was not broken up until 1929, though they heard on their return to Mudros that this attack had sunk another, much smaller, gunboat.

Later the same day an attack on a largish steamer had to be called off at the last moment when it was found that she was crowded with wounded. A tug towing three dhows each packed with wounded was also allowed to proceed unmolested.

> After tea Cochrane put a tea-leaf poultice on my left foot and a small one on the inside of my right leg. The rest of the right leg is dry and doing splendidly but there is still a slight discharge from the centre of the instep to the point of the heel and right up the leg to the top of the burns. Our medical book is of no help for it only gives directions for a couple of days' treatment "By which time of course the patient will have medical aid from the parent ship"!

The following day there was an ominous new development. Just before 1.0 pm Cochrane was called to the bridge when smoke was sighted on the port bow and they turned to investigate. As the minutes passed the target was seen to be a destroyer towing a submarine, at which time the *E7* dived as Cochrane hoped to gain an attacking position without being seen. But they had been seen, for the destroyer slipped the tow and began zig-zagging between the *E7's* diving position and the U-boat. The enemy was the *UB8* on its way to attack shipping off Mudros, but though von Voigt could count himself lucky to escape from Cochrane his patrol was unsuccessful. After firing his torpedoes, which failed to hit their targets, he returned to Constantinople with his batteries contaminated with sea water.

By contrast to the bad luck of the 13th, the 15th was to be a real red-letter day for the *E7*, not so much for its success but for the fact that this was the day they attacked the enemy in Constantinople. Nasmith had taken the *E11* there. Now it was to be Cochrane's turn to be able to view the enemy capital through his periscope.

They had surfaced early that morning off Oxia island, one of a group of small islands to the east of the City which were either uninhabited or used for summer residences by wealthy Turks and foreigners. The British Consul had had one such house before the war on nearby Halki. It was in the Consul's requisitioned villa that Lieutenant-General Townshend was to spend the remainder of the war in comparative luxury after the fall of Kut el Amara in 1916 – in vastly different conditions from those endured by other POWs in

Turkish hands. As Cochrane waited to close the capital it was a hot misty day with visibility not more than five miles, few clouds overhead and not a breath of wind. Off the Bosphorus, which runs from the Black Sea to the Marmara, and, like the Dardanelles, separates European from Asiatic Turkey, there are strong tides and eddies, as Nasmith had found during his visit. Now the *E7* was carried in towards Scutari Point – famous in an earlier war for the hospital where Florence Nightingale strove to alleviate the sufferings of the wounded British troops – and there grounded on the Leander shoal. To make matters worse there was a thick scum on the surface of the water which dried on the top lens of the periscope after it had been up for a few seconds, obscuring Cochrane's view. The *Goeben* and *Breslau* were not in sight, in fact there were no worthwhile targets in sight, yet they could not leave the area without some action. From a position where Europe and Asia are only about a mile apart Cochrane fired a torpedo at the Topkhana Arsenal where a large number of small craft lay alongside loading munitions for the front. No one aboard the *E7* could doubt that they had hit something for a long loud explosion was clearly heard and was greeted by a great cheer. Cochrane was too busy working the submarine back into deep water after being taken aground again for him to notice just what effect this had had at the Arsenal. Even so, Hallifax noticed 'that he looked awfully bucked and can't stop smiling'.

Leaving Constantinople astern they moved southwards to be in position to bombard the nearby powder mills at Zeitun that evening. After dark they surfaced and cautiously moved inshore with the gun's crew ready to open fire. The moment came when the mills were silhouetted by the light of a passing train and they rapidly fired 12 rounds, though apparently with little effect. The results of these two actions were perhaps minimal in themselves but they produced a reaction ashore out of all proportion to their worth. The Turkish capital had been attacked by a British submarine. Many Turks were convinced that the British fleet had at last broken through the Dardanelles and that this was but a foretaste of the bombardments to come. Many left the city for the believed safety of the surrounding countryside. The following morning the *E7* was once again on the surface off Oxia island from where Cochrane and Twyman could hear the sounds of gunfire coming from the direction of the city. Who was firing at whom, or why, has never been established.

These two actions off Constantinople might be considered as the climax of the patrol, although they still had more than two weeks in the Sea of Marmara before they could return. There were no large ships to be found and Cochrane had to be content with intercepting and sinking numerous small steamers and sailing craft.

We came up with a sailing vessel, manned by Greeks, and loaded with charcoal. Put a 2½ pound charge in aft which blew her stern off. She went down quick at first but got an air lock in the fore hold and remained with the bow sticking out of the water. We rammed her twice with no effect. Previous to the charge Cochrane had attempted to cut a hole in her side with our small axe to see if it were possible to sink a ship in this way, but the axe was too small and light.

... Overhauled a sailing ship, a one-masted vessel but larger than most brigantines we have met. Cochrane thinks she must be Black Sea trade, being quite a different build. She was loaded with hay like a Thames barge and we blew her up with a 2½ pound charge. She sank at once and left the haystack floating and burning merrily! We got some fresh chicken's eggs from her – a nice change from our own which are near the limit.

Trains then became targets for the submarine's gunners, for in several places the railway track ran close to the shore and was well within range.

17 July
Bombarded a cutting through which the railway runs. Here the railway runs from Constantinople to Ismid and then on into Asia Minor and is only single track, but the only one. Along this one line all the supplies and reinforcements from Asia Minor go to Constantinople. We hit the cutting alright but could not tell what damage we had done.

Later.
Cochrane saw a train – a long one with two engines – pull up before it got to the cutting so we had evidently blocked the line, even if only temporarily.

22 July
When we were here the other day firing at the cutting Cochrane noticed a short tunnel to the westward of it and he was keen to have a try at knocking that in, though it is very doubtful what effect a 6-pounder shell would have on earth. We were closing in to shoot at the tunnel when Cochrane saw a train coming along – quite a short one – so we opened fire.

161

They had just got the range, one shot just missing the funnel of the engine, when the train nipped into the tunnel.

It was not until Hallifax was serving in Australia with the RAN's flotilla of 'J' class submarines in 1919 that he heard more of this incident. This train had not been carrying ammunition, nor even Turkish reinforcements, but rather the surviving crew of the *AE2* with their guards. It was just as well that they had not had time to hit the train before it reached the safety of the tunnel, but even so the *E7* had been cursed bitterly by their fellow submariners.

Then Cochrane opened fire on a stone bridge which carries the railway across a small stream. We hit it several times but I think that our shells are too small to do much damage. We then retired to the westward to the accompaniment of a furious rattle of rifle fire, apparently as the result of our last visit the line is now well guarded. Twyman said it was one continuous rattle but never saw a splash or even heard a bullet, we were way out of range.

Both Hallifax and Mathews were still suffering badly from their burns, and continued to do so for the whole patrol and long after. The high ambient temperature and humidity coupled with a shortage of clean bandages and the lack of any suitable medication can hardly have helped recovery. They were perhaps fortunate that their wounds did not become seriously infected. Despite the pain and his lack of mobility there were small ways in which Hallifax could help out and these were eagerly seized upon.

While they were firing this morning I started fuzing another box of shell. We finished all the base-fuzed last week and are now using "time and percussion" fuze supplied at Harwich for use against Zeppelins, and we have to fit new fuzes ourselves. We can only do one box at a time (11 shells) as with this nose fuze in the lids won't close down. When I had done six shells we came to the bottom row of fuzes which we found to be "percussion" rather than "time and percussion". These fuzes were found to be about 1½ inches too long and not big enough diameter to screw in. We have only six rounds of shell left, the remainder can't be used.

Cochrane himself became unwell. On 20 July Hallifax recorded that his eyes were troubling him, that he was feverish and that he was having to dose himself with quinine. Not a happy position for any

16.   HMS *B6* off Cape Helles. Note the shell burst ashore.

17.   HMS *E7* in the anchorage at Mudros.

18. Lieutenant Gravener and the crew of HMS *B10* shortly after their patrol off Bodrum
Gravener is seated centre with woolly hat. The blurring to the right of Gravener's head
an effort by the censor to remove the tube containing the submarine's compass.

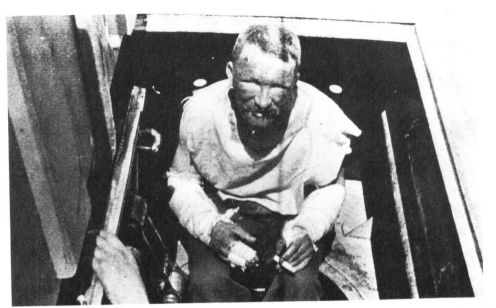

19. Able Seaman Mathews about to leave the *E7* after the return to Mudros from the Sea of Marmara. His arms and hands are still heavily bandaged as a result of the burns he received at the start of the patrol.

20. Commander Boyle, in long coat, bringing the *E14* to Malta. The strange-shaped submarine in the left background is one of the French boats.

21.   The Crew of HMS *E*7 after being captured.

22.   Cochrane (standing fourth from left) with other officers in Cyprus after their escape from
       Yozgad POW camp in 1918. The Turkish and German flags were taken from the captured
       boat in which they crossed to the island.

submarine Commanding Officer to be in while on patrol, but made worse by having his second-in-command incapacitated and his only other officer an inexperienced reservist. Only days later, having recovered from the fever, he was suffering badly from neuralgia though he tried to make light of the pain and remarked to Twyman, 'You can't gaze through glasses for up to 15 hours a day for three weeks without trouble cropping up'.

On 22 July they were expecting to meet up with the *E11* who would be coming up to relieve them. They had then been there for over three weeks and had not enough fuel left to last them for another week. Reaching the agreed rendezvous they steamed slowly on the surface so that the other submarine could see and close them. There was nothing else in sight for targets had become very few and far between and there were only the patrolling Turkish gunboats to worry about. At 4 o'clock that afternoon a submarine was sighted and three hours later the two boats came alongside one another in the lee of the shore to exchange news. The other boat was not the *E11*, which was only that day leaving Malta after a refit, but the *E14,* with Boyle, now a Commander, making his third patrol.

Boyle came across with instructions for the *E7's* return and to warn Cochrane about new nets which the Turks were laying across the Dardanelles at Nagara and which had first been sighted by seaplane patrols of the RNAS. Boyle himself had seen the buoys stretching about two-thirds of the way across, but had reached the Marmara without undue difficulty. He also warned Cochrane that the French submarine *Mariotte* would be attempting to join him in the Marmara as soon as she could be readied and that Cochrane should be careful before firing at strange submarines!

They also learnt that all their signals had indeed reached Keyes and that it was the *E7's* receiver that was at fault. This was something that he had suspected. One night when trying to contact the *Jed* he had in desperation suggested that a signal rocket be fired if they were receiving his signals and had been rewarded by the subsequent flare in the sky from over the peninsula.

Stanley [First Lieutenant of the E14] came across to see me. He told me that the Turks had announced that in view of the attacks by British submarines on harmless people they will send French and Englishmen now in their hands down into the war zone. Sir Edward Grey has replied that he will hold Enver Bey and others named personally responsible for them. The Turks have said no more. Sir Edward also warned them that they are suspected of sending troops down in steamers and sending the wounded back in the same ships and not announcing and painting the ships in accordance with the Hague Convention. He warned the Turks that they render themselves liable to attack. It is good to know that our doings here ARE noticed by the Turks.

Later.

When we got to the bottom Cochrane had all hands for'd and told them that we would be going out on Saturday morning. He said that unless anyone felt he could grow a decent beard, and wanted to, he was to shave before we got in. (This was a matter I had intended to speak about, for I want us to arrive looking less lousy than the usual style.) He added that with regard to letters they could say anything as long as they do not mention other boats and that he will pass their letters UNREAD if they undertake to do this. He is very cheery tonight.

In the short time left before they started to return through the Dardanelles there were no targets to attack. They spent one morning getting the gun and its mounting dismantled and stowed securely inside the casing so that it would not foul any nets or mine mooring wires. The battery was then fully charged and they were ready for the final stage.

At 6.30 am on Saturday 24 July they were off Gallipoli town, the E7 was dived and they headed southwards. Cochrane's own report is typically laconic, taking a mere 22 lines to tell the whole story, including the meeting with a north-bound destroyer which passed them unaware of their presence and too close for Cochrane to fire at. Hallifax gives more details.

9.40: Passed the nets off Nagara Point by keeping close to the shore. We are going slow past here as the periscope is continually being used and we don't want it to feather. There is a nice fresh NE breeze which makes it better for us as it ruffles the water.

10.50: We went on "passing" those nets for 30 minutes or so and at the bearing of Nagara Point remained on the port bow! At last we did get past the Point and altered course to the south though heaven knows what got hold of us all that time. Suddenly Cochrane saw a fresh line of buoys right across our track and not more than 100 yards away. We went to 90 feet but must have hit a net or something for we started to come up and had to let a lot of extra water into Y (compensating tank).

10.05: Rounded Kilid Bahr and shaped course S50W at 40 feet and the next minute the helmsman reported that the helm was hard-a-starboard★ and that the boat was still swinging to starboard. Then she started to come up. We flooded two more compensating tanks and she would only stay down with the motors stopped. We reversed the helm, ahead port, astern starboard and she turned right round. We had to stop port for that brought her up. Flooded in more water to the tanks and also to one of the fuel tanks and after 20 anxious minutes were suddenly able to steer and to keep depth. Cochrane says it was a mine which must have caught up forward somehow, though we heard nothing. He had begun to fear that we should have to wait for dark and then surface to clear it.

11.50: He ordered watch diving stations and passed the word to those aft that "we are now clear" and having given the coxswain a bottle of beer he opened one for himself. He had got half a glass poured when "Helm hard-a-port and still swinging to port" and then "She's coming up, Sir". Another mine caught? More turning and twisting, backing and filling to try and clear it. It took about 23 minutes and we could breath easily again. Later we caught another aft but dropped it almost at once. The battery could not have been fully charged last night as we thought for before we rounded Nagara we only had 85 volts on the lights with all resistance out. We switched off all but three groups but there was not sufficient light to see the chart and we had to light the emergency lamps on the gauges. By 2.0 o'clock the lights in the fore compartment were just glowing red and the compartment was virtually in darkness.

At 3.05 pm came to surface near Morto Bay. Tried to start the engine on air but they were reluctant to go so the motors gave them a hand. The lights went clean out with that load.

Escorted by a destroyer the *E7* made her way to Mudros where they passed the boom and entered the great harbour shortly after 7.0 pm. Hallifax was unable to witness the tumultuous reception they were given by the ships of the fleet and the transports which thronged the harbour, and the record in his diary relies mainly on Twyman's account of events.

Just outside the boom the escorting destroyer signalled to us: 'I ought to lead you in, but I would rather you led'. We shot clear while old Cochrane grinned and tried to make a suitable reply. Inside the boom we passed

---

★ The old style helm orders were still used whereby, as in the manner of a sailing ship, if the helm was put to starboard then the ship altered to port.

several big transports, small steamers and trawlers all crowded with troops on their way to the front. They gave us tremendous rounds of cheers, waving their rifles and hats, which Twyman said began to make him think a bit. Then appeared a boat with Brodie and several officers which dashed round us as they cheered and waved. That made Twyman think a bit more.

Then came a cheer from the AGAMEMNON, and after that a continuous roll of cheering from every ship in the harbour – even those at the end of the Bay. Twyman the cynic has changed! He said he felt like tears and had a lump in his throat, while his chest swelled with pride till it felt like bursting and when he looked at unemotional sphinx-like old Cochrane he had tears slowly trickling through his eyelashes.

Some brass-hatted individual (I found out later it was Admiral Gamble) came along to meet us in a steam picket boat, stopped almost ahead of us and got his boat's crew up to clap wildly. Our crew, in their excitement, waved back. The RELIANCE, crowded with dockyard mateys, let out a terrific 'Are we downhearted?' through a megaphone, and all the mateys answered with a loud 'No!'

So, after twenty-four days in the Sea of Marmara, the *E7* returned to Mudros as both the *E11* and *E14* had done before, having seriously interrupted enemy sea-borne traffic from Constantinople. Twyman, in writing of the patrol in a letter to his father, fairly sums up the momentous days:

Cochrane was absolutely splendid. The tale of our doings is the sort of thing one reads of in the old days. We went round the Sea of Marmara leaving a trail of sunk and burning ships. We fairly shook things to the core.

Even now it is difficult to assess just how much damage the *E7*, or any of the submarines, actually did during the patrols in the Sea of Marmara. Turkish records do not give this detail, while on the German side their official history tends to play down the part played by the Allied submarines. Altogether, it is believed that the *E7* accounted for one gunboat, five steamers including one of about 3,000 tons, and seventeen large sailing vessels, besides any lighters destroyed or damaged by the torpedo fired at the Arsenal in Constantinople and the damage to the railway system by their bombardments. It was a patrol in which Cochrane truly emulated the deeds of his famous ancestor.

Keyes recognized the worth of the patrol and believed that, like Boyle and Nasmith before him, Cochrane had earned a VC for his efforts, but, like almost everyone else, did not believe that he would be awarded one. In the event Cochrane received a DSO. Twyman was rewarded with a DSC while Petty Officer Websdale, the Coxswain, who had helped the two officers with some watch-keeping duties after Hallifax had gone sick and had been highly commended by Cochrane, received the DSM. Leading Seaman Dempsey who had been in charge of the gun's crew also received a DSM.

As the fighting ashore continued so did the submarine campaign in the Marmara. The *E14* had relieved the *E7*, the *E11* was back from refit in Malta and making ready to go on patrol again. The French too were eager to try and get one of their boats through the Dardanelles. As for the *E7* she was due for repairs in Malta before it would be her turn again, while for Hallifax and Mathews there were still many painful weeks ahead for them before they would be fit for duty again.

12

To The Dardanelles Again

FOR HALLIFAX AND for Mathews the return to Mudros meant proper medical attention at last and relief from the unhygienic conditions on the submarine. Even so, the conditions on the *Adamant* in Mudros – hot and humid – were not considered good for their swift recovery and it was hoped to send them to Malta, though the climate was little better there, but the hospitals were so full of wounded that they had to stay in Mudros. They were promised two weeks' sick leave there later when they were fit enough to travel. Meanwhile Hallifax tried to get away in the *Imogene*, a converted yacht, which ran back and forth to Athens, but getting permission to go and being able to catch the ship during her brief visits to Mudros were easier said than done.

The *E7*, however, did go to Malta to refit, sailing on 11 August. Meanwhile the *E2* had arrived from Harwich to swell the numbers of Allied submariners eager to try and gain glory in the Sea of Marmara. Profiting from the earlier experience of the *E14* and *E11* which had gone up first without guns and then, like the *E7*, with only a 6-pounder gun, she had been fitted with a 12-pounder.

On the return of the *E7* from their momentous patrol one of the first to call on Cochrane to hear of his experiences was the Commanding Officer of the French *Mariotte*, whose own departure had been specially postponed to allow this meeting. Sadly it was to no avail. The *Mariotte*, rather smaller than the British E class and built in 1911, got caught in the net off Nagara and, after struggling for some hours to free herself, had had to surface. When the crew had safely abandoned the boat she was scuttled. All but one of her crew were saved.

168

The British, with the arrival of the *E2* and the imminent departure from England of the *E20* with her massive 6-inch howitzer, were not the only side to send submarine reinforcements to the Mediterranean. The Germans sent three more of their small boats from Pola. The *UC15* (von Dewitz) was the first of this batch to leave on 7 July. With the *UC15* went urgent war supplies for the Turks, albeit in small quantities, and four spare torpedoes for the U-boats already in the Eastern Mediterranean. With these precious supplies on board, von Dewitz was warned to steer well clear of likely trouble, the more so as his small UC-type submarine was not fitted with torpedo tubes. He took nearly two weeks to reach the base at Bodrum, barely reaching harbour, with his engine broken and his batteries nearly exhausted. With the exception of the spare torpedoes and some bottles of acetone his cargo was unloaded and taken on fifty camels overland all the way to Constantinople while the boat was repaired. To hide her from the sight of any patrolling British submarine or from the eyes of agents on the many sailing vessels in the area she was placed on the bottom near the shore with only the top of her conning tower above water, while the small exposed area was carefully painted to blend with the colour of the shore. Von Dewitz and his crew then disembarked to wait for the arrival of skilled help from the *Goeben* to effect repairs. It was 9 August before the *UC15* was ready to sail again.

The *UB14* (von Heimburg) followed, leaving Pola on 15 July. She too went first to Bodrum, arriving at about the same time as the *E7* was arriving in triumph at Mudros; she too was in a poor mechanical state on arrival and required time before being considered fit to go to sea again. When she did next sail on 13 August it was not long before she was to strike a tragic blow at the reinforcements arriving for the Allied armies in Gallipoli. Von Heimburg planned to attack ships which were on their way to Lemnos from Alexandria and which passed all too close to the German-Turkish base. The first night out he watched unobserved as a brightly lit hospital ship went by, to be rewarded the following morning. Just before 9 o'clock a large unescorted troopship came into sight from the southward and within half an hour von Heimburg had fired a single torpedo from an ideal position on the beam at the comparatively long range of 1750 yards. The torpedo exploded right aft on the 11000-ton troopship *Royal Edward* and she sank rapidly stern first taking with her nearly 900 officers and men of the embarked troops and crew. The *UB14* returned to Bodrum.

A signal came in to say that the ROYAL GEORGE, a big transport, had been torpedoed and sunk – to the east of the Duoro Sound I believe. The SUDAN is standing by and the GLOUCESTER CASTLE, another hospital ship, is hastening to the rescue.

Saturday 14 August.
Unless there are two transports named ROYAL GEORGE there must be some mistake in the name reported yesterday. The officers of the E14 declare that they passed the ROYAL GEORGE on their way into harbour yesterday – and read her name on the stern.

16 August. (While visiting the yacht SUNBEAM, converted to a hospital ship by Lord and Lady Brassey who remained on board.)
About eight patients arrived after tea, three of them survivors from the ROYAL EDWARD. She sank in about five minutes. The SUDAN picked up 400 and a number got away in boats but I am afraid about a thousand must have drowned. Only one of the survivors appeared to be wounded and he had his neck bandaged, also his right eye. His face was badly bruised, I rather think a rope having caught him.

At this time the *UB8* left the Dardanelles to attack shipping off the landing beaches at Suvla Bay, but von Voigt missed his targets in two attacks and then had to return with damage to his battery which was giving off chlorine gas. The *UC15* was able to complete her passage to Constantinople while the *UB14* left Bodrum again on 18 August to see if there were promising targets off the Dardanelles. The third of the reinforcing boats left Pola when the *UC13* (Kirchner) sailed with another 30 tons of war stores embarked.

Off the Dardanelles the *UB14* became caught in a net and von Heimburg tried for hours to free the boat before succeeding. Once more he went back to Bodrum where a wire which had become jammed between the propeller and the stern gland had to be cut free by men with diving gear. Soon after leaving finally for the Dardanelles, he found another unescorted troopship, the *Southland*, at which he fired a torpedo from 1400 yards' range. Although the torpedo hit, with the loss of a number of lives, the troops were disembarked and the *Southland* limped into Mudros where she was beached. Among the ships taking off the troops from the *Southland* was HMS

Ben-my-Chree, once an Isle of Man ferry but now one of the early seaplane carriers with the fleet off the Dardanelles.

2 September
In the evening the BEN-MY-CHREE came in crowded with troops from the SOUTHLAND followed by a similarly laden French destroyer, and then another transport came in with more troops who might have been survivors, but I could not make sure. I don't think there can have been many casualties.

3 September
The SOUTHLAND was brought in and beached, which was good. Casualties about 70.

The *E7* was due to return to the Sea of Marmara in early September. She had returned from her refit in Malta on 25 August with Cochrane, as usual, anxious to sail before all the refit work was completed and concerned that the *E12*, with her even bigger 4-inch gun, would be selected for the next patrol ahead of him.

It had been a fantastic race between E7 and E12 as to which would get out first and so get up the hole next. E12 was going out, firing her 4 inch, diving, rushing back into harbour to have leaking rivets caulked and then dashing out again for more trials. E7 left (as usual) with both engines in pieces; the dockyard was repairing the port circulating pump and Cochrane chucked the "Maties" out in a hurry, with the result that one went away in a hurry with the oil rings in his pocket and they could do nothing more in the way of finishing it off during the trip. Outside the harbour they proceeded on motors for some time before the engines (or rather, one) could be made to start, and later they started the other. There was evidently a water service leak somewhere for when it started there was a bang as one piston broke and its connecting rod bent. They had to lash that piston up. They nearly came the whole way on one engine as the pump would not keep both cool. Now of course there is four days' work to get ready again for sea. It is absurd this sort of thing, the ERAs were tired out when they left Malta, and now after this trip, during which they have never ceased working, they are hard at it again.

30 August
The E7 is getting all ready to go up now, her engine is nearly finished and Cochrane expects to go this week. The crew have been digging out all day drawing 350 rounds of Lyddite and then hoisted in her final torpedoes. The boat is now chock-a-block with torpedoes and ammunition.

31 August

E7 goes from here on Thursday. Cochrane got a dozen bombs from the Army ammunition ship today; lovely little things.

For Hallifax it must have been galling to watch all these preparations and know that he would not be fit to go with the boat. His friend John Scaife had been appointed as First Lieutenant in his stead. The only question to be resolved was his own future; his burnt legs still had not healed properly and there was little strength in the legs themselves. As he was then about next in line for his own command it seemed that one solution would be to send him home to recuperate properly and then to be re-appointed.

1 September

Went over to the PRINCE GEORGE with the Doctor from the ADAMANT this morning and at about 10 o'clock went before the Board which consisted of the DGI, a Fleet and a Staff Surgeon. They started reading my papers, asked me how long since the burns occurred and told me to get my bandages off. While I was doing this the Doctor, in answer to a question, said that my skin was very thin and that a submarine was a bad place for me at present and for some time to come. When I had got half the right bandage off the DGI said that he thought it was unnecessary to look at my legs as it rather cast aspersions on my Doctor's ability. But the Staff Surgeon said in a very determined voice, "No, Sir, I want to see it", so they had to. As soon as the lint came off they all jumped up, then sat down together and said "Home" in decided tones, and that finished the proceedings.

At 9.30 pm I got a signal ordering me to sail in the HUNTSEND tomorrow forenoon – a blooming collier I believe, but I'll take mighty good care to get out of her at Malta and see if I can do the rest of the way in style.

2 September

After breakfast I found that the HUNTSEND is the ex-LUTZOW, one of the Norddeutcher Lloyd's China boats. She and her sister ship, the DERFLINGER, were captured at the beginning of the war and are now both used as transports. When I got on board no one knew anything about me, but I got a berth in a cabin, the other occupant being a Lieutenant-Commander RNVR – a dysentery case. Before I left the ADAMANT I saw a wireless message that the SOUTHLAND had been torpedoed only about 20 miles south of Lemnos – that sounded very nice for us!

Later

The ship is full of wounded with 11 doctors and 14 nurses, it would be an awful show if we were torpedoed. On account of Fritz we did not sail at 7.0 pm but will probably sail tomorrow.

From the *Adamant*, where he was packing his kit and making his farewells before going aboard the *Huntsend*, Hallifax watched the *E7* leave the anchorage at Mudros for the advanced base at Kephalo Bay on Imbros. From there Cochrane would be able to fly over the Dardanelles in one of the RNAS seaplanes to observe the latest state of the defences. Then, at 2 am on 4 September, Cochrane took the *E7* to sea to head once again for the Sea of Marmara. Before the day was out the *E7* would be no more, having been caught in the great net at Nagara. In contrast to their first trip up the Dardanelles the night was very calm and there was a bright moon, so when abeam of Achi Baba, Cochrane dived to avoid being seen from the shore and alerting the defences, and then passed under the minefield. By 6.30 they were off the fort at Kilid Bahr, but their periscope was seen and fired on. Then an hour later they came up to the net at Nagara.

Long after the war Petty Officer Sims, by then a retired Chief Petty Officer, could still vividly remember the events of the next few hours. Throughout the length of the submarine each man was at his action station, though it seems that at least some of them who were not actively engaged in working the submarine were trying to relax or were even playing cards in an effort to forget the tension as they headed towards the most dangerous part of the whole passage. Sims, as the senior torpedoman, was also the electrician and his duty was in the motor room. After Cochrane had ordered full speed on both motors he headed towards the net at a depth of 100 feet. All at once there was a terrific jolt as if the boat had run aground. The shock flung men off-balance, while seconds later another shock completed the confusion. The net had caught them, stretched, and then actually flung them astern despite the power of the motors. Although the bows had in fact forced their way partially through the net the submarine was firmly held.

Cochrane himself remained cool and unperturbed in the face of this setback. His own report, admittedly not written until after the war, is typically laconic:

Sighted the buoys of the submarine net off Nagara Point and altered course to cross the net at right angles. Dived to 100 feet and increased speed to 7½ knots. Shortly after the boat reached 100 feet and at the moment that the bows were heard to cut through the net the starboard propeller fouled and stopped the motor. The port motor was immediately increased to full speed, and as the boat's head fell off to port the helm was put hard over until at the end of ten minutes, by which time the starboard propeller was clear, the boat was lying on the northern side of the net parallel to and much entangled with it. In order to keep the propellers clear of the net I decided to turn the boat's head to the southward and pass through the net. Then at 8.30 a mine exploded a few hundred feet from the boat, no damage being done.

After about two hours' manoeuvring the boat was turned to the south, and repeated attempts to clear the net were made at depths from 60 to 130 feet by going alternatively full speed ahead and full speed astern. Although several meshes of the net were carried away it was impossible to gather sufficient way to clear completely the many parts which were holding the boat fore and aft.

10.30 am. Another mine exploded close to the boat. The explosion was violent but no damage done to the hull. After this explosion the boat was considerably freer than before, and in the hopes that further attempts to blow up the boat might result in completely freeing her, I decided to remain submerged at a good depth till after dark, when it might be possible to come to the surface and clear the obstruction.

Burned all confidential papers.

By 2.0 pm the battery power was much reduced and further attempts to get clear were given up for the time.

Not only was the battery power much reduced, but there were problems with the starboard motor where the starting resistances had become badly overheated. Small drops of molten copper sprayed out every time the motor was started, some falling on a bale of cotton waste cleaning material which started a small fire. Chief Petty Officer Jack Harrison, the chief engine room artificer, and two stokers soon had the blaze out but the residual smoke did little to help the already foul atmosphere. It was as well that they did act quickly for Sims clearly remembered his fears as he stood at the switchboard and saw the flames much too close for safety to some of the cases of explosives which were stowed throughout the boat ready for use on enemy shipping when they reached the Sea of Marmara. For some time the situation remained quiet, Cochrane content to let the hours slip by until darkness, while, unknown to him, the enemy prepared the next move.

6.40 pm: A mine exploded only a few feet from the hull. The explosion was very violent, electric light and other small fittings were broken. The motors were at once started in the hope that the net had been destroyed, but this was not the case. The presence of enemy craft on the surface made it impossible to come to the surface after dark and so clear the obstruction. I decided to come at once to the surface and remove the crew from the boat before blowing her up.

The boat was brought to the surface without difficulty.

John Scaife, the new First Lieutenant, who had been born in Constantinople and could speak Turkish, was the first out of the conning tower waving a white tablecloth to surrender the boat, emerging to a hail of fire from machine guns both from ashore and from the small flotilla of motor boats which surrounded the striken submarine. Luckily he was unscathed, and the firing died down once the initial excitement caused by the appearance of the submarine had died down. Then the boats came alongside to take off the submarine's crew. Up they came, one by one, and stepped unhindered into the boats, among them Chief Stoker Asher Coates, one of the card players when they had first hit the net, and who was not to survive the Turkish POW camps; Able Seaman "Johno" Johnson, the boat's mascot, who had already survived the sinking of the *Hogue*, to be rescued by the *Cressy*, only to be a survivor a second time within the hour when that ship too was sunk; Leading Stoker Wilson who couldn't swim, despite all their efforts to teach him, and who was told that this was an adjectival good chance to learn now; and Able Seaman Reid, ever the humourist, who like Coates would not survive the rigours of captivity. Cochrane himself was the last up from below, having opened the vents to the ballast tanks to dive the boat and then fired the fuses to the scuttling charges. He was the only one to get wet for as he prepared to jump the submarine began to settle and he had to be dragged aboard the Turkish motor boat. He had hoped that the explosion of the charges as the submarine sank would tear great holes in the net which would not be repaired before the next boat tried to get through into the Marmara. However, it is possible that though some charges went off the main charge did not; perhaps the inrush of water down the conning tower displaced some of the fuses. In any event the E7 went to the bottom, leaving the net largely in place.

Cochrane complimented his crew on their behaviour during the long trying hours that they had been caught in the net:

> The discipline and behaviour of the crew was excellent; this was particularly noticeable at the time of the third explosion. At this time the crew had been fallen out, and many were asleep. On being called to their stations every man went quietly to his place though the violence of the explosion was such as to convince everyone that the boat was badly damaged. It was only after receiving the various reports that the bilges were dry that I was able to realize that the hull had not received serious damage.

It is interesting to speculate on what Cochrane had planned for this patrol. Shipping of any size in the Sea of Marmara was by then even scarcer than on their first patrol, while the smaller ships tended to be well escorted. Obviously the gun with its ample supply of ammunition would have been an important asset. Commodore Keyes in his own Memoirs makes the intriguing statement: 'Before leaving, Cochrane discussed with me a plan for inflicting damage in the Golden Horn, which for ingenuity rivalled the most brilliant of his grandfather's exploits'. Unfortunately, it seems that nowhere is there a record of what this plan involved; moreover Keyes apparently did not ask any other Commanding Officer proceeding into the Marmara to attempt it. There are, perhaps, some clues.

In August Short 184 seaplanes from the *Ben-my Chree* had carried out the first aircraft-delivered torpedo attack. Nevertheless, even with the puny warhead of a 14-inch Mark X torpedo of 1897 vintage, its total weight of 762 pounds, taken together with the weight of the aircraft's fuel, made take-off difficult in all but ideal conditions and then only with enough range for a short sortie. Perhaps it was thought that this range could be significantly increased if a submarine were to carry extra fuel to refuel the aircraft near to its target, say in the Sea of Marmara. Or, alternatively, if the aircraft took off with a full fuel tank from Imbros or the Gulf of Xeros then it could be given its weapons, either torpedo or bombs, in the Sea of Marmara from the submarine.

Such a scheme had been put forward by John Porte early in the war. He had been one of the first pilots in the RNAS before being invalided from the service before the war and going to work in America for one of the then emerging aircraft companies. Returning to Britain on the outbreak of war he had not only rejoined the RNAS but also persuaded the Admiralty to buy the two flying boats in which he had been planning to attempt to cross the Atlantic. Porte was stationed at Felixstowe and he envisaged the flying boats crossing the North Sea and meeting one of the Harwich-based submarines off Heligoland to take on fuel or bombs before taking off again to attack the German fleet bases. No doubt that during his time in Harwich Cochrane had heard of this scheme, though the weather conditions in the North Sea were hardly suitable. It would have seemed more feasible in the Mediterranean, especially after the generally calm conditions met with in the Sea of Marmara during the *E7's* patrol.

John Hart was serving in the *Ben-my-Chree* at that time as a civilian volunteer, in the same way that the *Sarnia* had a largely merchant navy crew to do non-naval tasks. He has recorded that on 3 September when both the *Ben-my-Chree* and the *E7* were in Kephalo Bay on Imbros Island the submarine had gone alongside the carrier and embarked a load of aircraft fuel. It sounds a dangerous cargo for the *E7* to have embarked and there is no mention of whether this was in one of the submarine's tanks or in cans stowed either internally or externally. It would probably not have been possible to embark torpedoes inside the hull but they could have been placed inside the casing, though bombs would have been more easily handled. In any event, we do know that one of the *Ben-my-Chree's* aircraft was lowered on to the foredeck of the *E7* while she lay alongside.

In an experiment early in 1915 the German *U9* had carried a seaplane on her casing off the Flanders coast, launching it for take-off by trimming down, the idea being to extend the aircraft's range by carrying it on the submarine towards its target, in this case the mouth of the River Thames. The experiment was not a success, marred mainly by unsuitable sea conditions, again something which would not necessarily be the case in the Sea of Marmara.

Cochrane's actual plan remains a mystery. Whatever he planned for the seaplane, it is unlikely that he would have been content for the *E7* to play the passive role of a submersible garage. Perhaps he planned a combined attack in conjunction with the seaplane on Constantinople where the *Goeben* and *Breslau* lay near the Golden Horn.

The architect of the final explosion that ended any hope for the *E7* was none other than von Heimburg of the *UB14*. His boat had arrived at Chanak from Bodrum that very day. Learning of the drama taking place only a few miles away he arranged for explosive charges to be disembarked from the U-boat and taken to the scene with some of his crew. Von Heimburg himself ensured that Cochrane and his men were well treated, at least until they reached Constantinople.

The *E7* was no more and the war was over for Cochrane and his crew. They all survived the sinking of the submarine; sadly not all survived the grim conditions of Turkish POW camps. The campaign on the Gallipoli peninsula was to continue until the early days of 1916. It seems strange that after all the lost chances of the entire operation the final evacuations were not only well planned but were executed without a single casualty. The last man left the peninsula on the night of 8/9 January.

With the final withdrawal of the troops from the tip of the peninsula at Cape Helles, there was no need for further attempts on the Dardanelles by the submariners. The last submarine, the *E2*, was recalled from the Sea of Marmara on 2 January, 1916. Until then the submarines continued to give the greatest support to the army, dominating the scene in the inland sea. Such success was not achieved without further loss. The *Turquoise* became the only French submarine to break through the Dardanelles into the Marmara, but unfortunately within days ran ashore and was captured. To make matters worse her crew abandoned ship in haste, leaving vital papers to be seized and read by the exultant Germans. Among them were details of a rendezvous with the *E20*. The appointment was kept by the ubiquitous *UB14* and the British boat fell an easy victim to von Heimburg's torpedo.

The statistics of the campaign speak eloquently for the success of the submariners' efforts. The passage of the Dardanelles was successfully effected on nearly thirty occasions by the Allied submariners; Nasmith in the *E14*, who like Boyle carried out three patrols, spent over a hundred days in the Marmara. Between them, they frustrated the Turkish attempts to supply their troops by sea, sinking over 300 large and small vessels, steam and sail. In addition two battleships, a destroyer and five gunboats were sent to the bottom.

Hallifax, saddened by the news of the loss of the *E7*, which he heard on board the *Huntsend* when only one day out from Plymouth, reached there on the 18th.

Announced that the E7 has been lost and the crew captured; poor old boat, I am sorry about it. I am so sorry for Cochrane especially, and for poor old

Scaife who was so awfully keen to do a trip. I wonder if she was sunk going up and, if so, whether the battery gave out.

After his arrival he was examined by yet another Board of Doctors who sent him on sick leave during which time he got married and endured one of the early Zeppelin raids on London while on honeymoon in the Waldorf Hotel. In November, 1915, he joined HMS *Dolphin* at Gosport to take command of the old submarine *B5* which was employed on training duties. Then in October, 1916, he was appointed to the command of the *D7*, one of a number of submarines forming a flotilla based in Ireland on HMS *Vulcan* and commanded by the redoubtable Nasmith, by then a Captain.

In July, 1917, he was on patrol off the south-west coast of Ireland and was in the area when the Danish merchant ship *Ceres* was torpedoed and sunk. He actually saw the U-boat responsible, *U88*, commanded by Walther Schwieger who in the *U20* had sunk the *Lusitania*, but was unable to close and attack before the enemy had disappeared. Two days later the *U66* only escaped the *D7's* attentions by making a violent course alteration, leaving Hallifax to fire two torpedoes at long range on the quarter.

It was in September, 1917, when on patrol off the West coast of Ireland, that Hallifax sighted and torpedoed the *U45* in an attack which took only twenty-two minutes. Two survivors were picked up. Later the same day another submarine was sighted at which Hallifax fired another torpedo, but this time the range was long and the track angle poor. Not suprisingly he missed. The second submarine was the *U54*. For this attack Hallifax was awarded the DSO.

After the war Hallifax went out to Australia with the 'J' class submarines which made up the reformed Australian submarine flotilla. Later he commanded the submarine depot ship *Lucia* and its flotilla of submarines before a series of staff appointments brought his naval career to an end. He was recalled for service during the Second World War but retired again in 1946.

Cochrane and his crew were taken to Constantinople after their capture and locked up in the local prison along with common criminals. Eventually they were sent to POW camps, Cochrane going to Kara Hissar, situated in the middle of Asia Minor about 130 miles from the nearest coast with wild country intervening. In March, 1916,

Cochrane, with Lieutenant-Commander Stoker, who had commanded the *AE2*, and a Lieutenant Price, escaped. They travelled through
the Taurus Mountains towards the coast but after eighteen days their
strength was nearly gone, they were starving and their boots were in
tatters. Almost within sight of the sea they decided they had to ask for
help at a goatherd's hut and despite their pathetic condition tried to
pass themselves off as German surveyors! They were betrayed and
recaptured. Taken back to Constantinople they were held for six
months in solitary confinement before being brought before a Court
Martial. Extraordinarily, they were then sentenced to twenty-five
days imprisonment! It was to be another five months before they were
released to go to another POW camp.

Along with a number of army officers, most of whom had been
captured at Kut-el-Amara and had refused to give their parole not to
escape, Cochrane arrived in a camp at Yozgad in April, 1918. It was
situated deep in the heart of the Anatolian Mountains some 4500 feet
above sea level in rugged and forbidding terrain. Yozgad means 100
springs but there was little picturesque about the place, and for most of
the year the river was merely a shallow and dirty stream.

By various means the prisoners had managed to get information out
of the camp and Cochrane arranged for a boat to be offshore on a
particular stretch of the coast near Cyprus during the last days of
August, 1918. On the night of 7/8 August twenty-six prisoners in four
parties escaped from the camp. Cochrane's group, which was the
largest, headed for the rendezvous but they realized that they had not
left themselves sufficient time because the escape had had to be
delayed. The other three parties were all recaptured within days, but
Cochrane's group struggled on, overcoming incredible difficulties. It
is obvious from accounts of this journey that one person was the man
who kept them going – Cochrane. The threat of betrayal was always
near, they had to contend with armed brigands and overcome
shortage of food and water while coping with the rigours of the
mountains.

Eventually they reached the coast and then had to find a way out of
Turkey to Cyprus. Again it was Cochrane, a seaman once more, who
found the way. He swam out to hijack a small motor boat that had
anchored nearby, brought it back for his companions to board and
with the aid of a dinghy rowed out to sea before starting the engine.
The journey to Cyprus was not all plain sailing for they had to contend

with frequent stoppages of the engine. Often it ran for only a few moments at a time. But Cyprus was safely reached and they were all sent home to England where they had a final reunion dinner in London. It was Armistice Night!

For this escape Cochrane was awarded a bar to the DSO he had won for his patrol in the *E7* in the Sea of Marmara. In 1922 he resigned from the Navy and, like his famous ancestor, went in for politics. He became the MP for East Fife and later for Dumbartonshire. Then in 1936 came yet another change. It might be said that again he was following his ancestor for he went abroad, though in this case in the service of his own country for he was appointed Governor of Burma. It was a post he held until 1941 when he returned and rejoined the Navy for service during the Second World War. Like Hallifax he retired again once the war was over and died in 1958 at the age of 73.

Sources

At the Public Record Office:
  ADM 137/225   Eighth Submarine Flotilla, Reports and Memoranda to December 1914
  ADM 137/2067 Submarine attached to *HMS Maidstone*, Reports of Proceedings, 1914
  ADM 137/2068 Submarines attached to HMS Maidstone, Reports of Proceedings, 1915.
  ADM 137/2077 Submarine Patrol Reports, Dardanelles and Aegean
  ADM 173/1196 Log of *HMS E7* for July 1914
  ADM 196/49   } Officers' Records
  ADM 196/52   }

At the Naval Historical Library:
  Naval Staff Monographs, Home Waters Volumes 1 to 4 (To July 1915)
  Naval Staff Monograph, The Mediterranean (excluding the Dardanelles) 1914 and 1915.
  History of British Minefields, 1914–18.
  German History of the Naval War, War in Turkish Waters Vol 1. (trans).

At the Imperial War Museum:
  Diary of Commander Cecil Talbot, *HMS E6*
  Diary of Lieutenant Oswald Hallifax, *HMS E7*

At the RN Submarine Museum:
  Diaries, photographs and letters.

Bibliography

C. Aspinall-Oglander, *Roger Keyes*, Hogarth Press, 1951

C. G. Brodie, *Forlorn Hope*, Frederick Books, 1956

E. Bush, *Gallipoli*, Allen and Unwin, 1975

A. Cochrane, *The Fighting Cochranes*, Quiller Press, 1983

Sir Julian Corbett, *History of the Great War, Naval Operations, Volume II*, Longmans, Green and Co, 1921

A. B. Cunningham, *A Sailor's Odyssey*, Huchinson and Co Ltd, 1951

M. Gilbert, *Winston S. Churchill, Volume III 1914–16*, William Heinemann, 1971

J. Goldrick, *The King's Ships were at Sea*, USNI Press, 1984

B. Von O Groos, *Der Krieg Zur See: Nordsee Vol I, II and III*, E S Mittler & Sohn, Berlin, 1920

Paul G. Halpern (Ed), *The Keyes Papers*, Volume I 1914–18, Navy Records Society, 1972

R. Hough, *The Great War at Sea*, Oxford University Press, 1983

M. Johnston & K. Yearsley, *Four-Fifty Miles to Freedom*, William Blackwood and Sons, 1919

P. K. Kemp (Ed), *The Fisher Papers*, Volume I, Navy Records Society, 1960

R. Keyes, *The Naval Memoirs of Admiral of the Fleet, Sir R Keyes*, Thornton Butterworth Ltd, 1934

J. Laffin, *Damn The Dardanelles: The Story of Gallipoli*, Osprey Publishing Ltd, 1980

A. J. Marder, *From the Dreadnought to Scapa Flow* Vol II, Oxford University Press, 1965

R. McLaughlin, *The Escape of the Goeben*, Seeley Service, 1974

BIBLIOGRAPHY

A. Moorehead, *Gallipoli*, Hamish Hamilton, 1956

A. Temple Patterson, *Tyrwhitt of the Harwich Force*, Weidenfield and Nicolson

S. Roskill, *Hankey, Man of Secrets*. Volume I, 1877–1918, Collins, 1970

S. Roskill, *Churchill and the Admirals*, Collins, 1977

P. Shankland & A Hunter, *Dardanelles Patrol*, William Collins, 1964

A. Spindler, *Der Krieg Zur See: Der Handelskreig mit U-Booten*, Vol I & II, 1932

H. G. Stoker, *Straws in the Wind*, Herbert Jenkins Ltd, 1925

J. Terraine, *The First World War, 1914–1918*, Macmillan, 1965

Dan Van der Vat, *The Ship that Changed the World*, Hodder & Stoughton, 1985

J. Winton, *The Victoria Cross at Sea*, Michael Joseph, 1978

Index

In general, officers are indexed under the rank held when first mentioned. The names of Turkish and Russian warships are those used in Conway's *All the World's Fighting Ships, 1906–21*. Turkish place names are those given in the Admiralty Black Sea Pilot, or the Naval Intelligence Division's Geographical Handbook series, Turkey Volume I.